# DOES WOMAN EXIST?

# DOES WOMAN EXIST?

## BY
## DARÍO SALAS SOMMER

Edited by the Editorial Staff of the John Baines Institute, Inc.

1ˢᵗ Edition 2010

Published by
John Baines Institute, Inc
P.O. Box 8556 * F.D.R. Station * New York, NY 10150
www.ihpusa.org
ihpbooks@gmail.com

*Does Woman Exist?*
Originally published as: "**Existe la Mujer**"
By Darío Salas Sommer (aka John Baines)
Translated from Spanish by AJ and GI
Cover art by CH
Copyright 2010 by John Baines

ISBN: 978-1-882692-08-8
Library of Congress Control Number: 2010922020
1st Edition 2010

Published by John Baines Institute, Inc.
Printed in the United States of America

# Table of Contents

# PREFACE

This is not a book of formulas or recipes on how to become more feminine. Instead, it is directed toward women in the hope they will apply their individual sense of judgment and criteria to comprehend its message.

It is not feasible to change one's nature using a standard recipe that dispenses advice about what to do and what not to do. Change can only occur when one uses one's faculty of human intelligence, which when used authentically, produces a profound and definitive change in the inner world of the human being. This is what profound comprehension entails. Unfortunately, many people do not truly understand the meaning of comprehension, confusing it with a merely intellectual assertion. Without real comprehension taking place, it is normal to think that one knows something fully when in reality only the surface is known. All too often, people avoid profound reflection, preferring the superficial, trivial, or unimportant. This is precisely why many prefer to follow formulas or rigid guidelines and tools that indiscriminately pretend to substitute for one's sense of judgment and discernment.

Consumerism has also invaded the way in which human intelligence works in that many people naively believe ready-made solutions can replace mature consciousness.

It is important to clarify that the manipulation of human behavior does not represent development or growth, but is merely a substitute for change. When a person behaves according to external recommendations without using inner judgment or including the participation and direction of the "I," a person does not gain, but loses. Additionally, nothing new is contributed to a person regarding development. One behavior simply replaces another.

When an individual's "I" is a self-reflecting and conscious entity, it is able to regulate and direct the processes of introspection, analysis and judgment and it is also able to assure one's effective development without using standard recipes. Instead, the individual who possesses such an "I" will employ personal criteria in an increasingly more sensible and appropriate manner.

Recipes are similar to techniques used to train animals. Indeed, it is possible to train a dog to attack but it is difficult to teach it to discern between the objects of its attack—a bone, a delinquent or an honest man.

The love of recipes also indicates the aversion people have for making decisions and for being responsible for their own actions, preferring instead to submit to external recommendations that do not require much profound thought.

The average person cannot even conceive the immense power that exists within real comprehension. The power of comprehension is so important that it generates essential changes in the thinker when something is truly understood at a most profound level. The individual who upon profound reflection is able to penetrate and understand the transcendence of truth and significance can modify his/her internal nature, and in so doing, develop a mature "I"—the only authentic source of freedom and self-determination.

To try to mold women by giving them a model of prefabricated femininity can be considered a lack of respect for them as individuals. Therefore, one must hope that women will take up the task of self-fulfillment on their own, through self-study, through the need to grow as individuals within their own personal styles but according to certain guidelines.

It is paramount that women study and understand their real situation on their own, not by emotionally adhering to a feminist movement or similar group. It is possible that the guidelines offered to women in this book—which are technical and concrete—might seem shocking. These guidelines are neither romantic nor persuasive. They do not seek to qualify or disqualify the feminine sex. On the contrary, I am guided to help women understand their most profound motivations. If it is necessary to expose unhealthy or inadequate behavior for a woman's individual development, it must be done because otherwise that behavior will hinder the possibility for growth. I hope that the reader therefore comprehends that this work is not guided by criticism; its purpose is technical and curative.

Femininity today is ill and the cure is painful. All change and growth by nature includes a measure of pain. Only those women who freely wish to heal, having recognized their behavior in the pages that follow, will be able to do so. In reality, a woman cannot try to achieve full femininity without the authentic development of her "I."

Perhaps the most difficult ordeal for a human being is to recognize and accept one's own defects which are often experienced as humiliating and offensive and are seldom considered a prerequisite to growth. People are susceptible to criticism because it is perceived as an attack and produces emotionally aggressive reactions instead of analysis without prejudice. This attitude can be compared to a person who dislikes his or her own image and fights with the mirror. A healthier kind of behavior would be to change the image, instead of denying the evidence!

It is natural to have defects; we all have them. To recognize them, accept them and become responsible for them is a pre-requisite for personal development because without such an honest and courageous act one can only cling blindly to an idealized structure and deny change.

Some might be tempted to label me a chauvinist instead of honestly seeing the evidence shown here. For all eternity, people have tended to use the unconscious trick of disqualifying or discrediting any individuals who uncover concepts that threaten their self-esteem rather than trying to evaluate the same concepts through the use of logical reasoning.

It is the individual who suffers irreparable loss when employing such an unconscious mechanism for one would be closing the door to knowledge that is vital and absolutely necessary for progress, well-being, and development.

The purpose of these reflections is to alert one to the uselessness of avoiding unpleasant experiences by taking refuge in pleasant illusions. When such a practice becomes habitual, a person's individual consciousness will start to deteriorate.

Understanding that there are impediments to women's self-fulfillment should not be considered offensive. Instead, it indicates that there is an authentic possibility to reach total feminine development.

Once again, I must insist that there needs to be a profound comprehension of women's hidden motivations. Such comprehension is a pre-requisite for the process of change that must then begin.

Many women have asked why I did not write a book entitled *Does Man Exist?* Firstly, such a question is defensive, not constructive. Its aim is not to aid a woman's development but rather to defend against men. But the answer is obvious: men have nothing to do with the development of women; women can grow without asking permission from the opposite sex.

The same is true of questions such as: "Why does a man have to come and show us what being a woman is?" or "How can a man *know* what a woman is like?" Since the ability to use one's intelligence abstractly has no gender, provided one describes another human being objectively and without prejudice, there should be no obstacles to the truth.

Anyone can feel attacked or criticized but when an argument is posed constructively and is adequately supported with proof, denial or rationalization will only constitute the loss of a great opportunity.

Darío Salas Sommer

# INTRODUCTION

Throughout the ages, women have been considered inferior to men and have been held in a subordinate, passive, and limited position. Women have not had equality with men.

In December 1979, the United Nations (UN) recognized the seriousness of this position, and approved the *Convention on the Elimination of all Forms of Discrimination against Women* (CEDAW). Adopted by the UN General Assembly in December of that year, it was the result of five years of research by several working groups with the commission for women's legal and social rights at the UN. CEDAW is often described as an international bill of rights for women. It consists of a preamble and 30 articles, and it defines what constitutes discrimination against women, setting up an agenda for international action to end such discrimination.

The Convention defines discrimination against women as "...any distinction, exclusion or restriction made on the basis of sex which has the effect or purpose of impairing or nullifying the recognition, enjoyment or exercise by women, irrespective of their marital status, on a basis of equality of men and women, of human rights and fundamental freedoms in the political, economic, social, cultural, civil or any other field."

It calls for the approval of multi-national laws that will forbid discrimination, recommends special temporary measures to accelerate equality *de facto* between men and women, and introduces devices to modify socio-cultural patterns that perpetuate discrimination.

It later adds:

"Affirming that the strengthening of international peace and security, the relaxation of international tension, mutual co-operation among all states irrespective of their social and economic systems, general and complete disarmament, in particular nuclear disarmament under strict and effective international control, the affirmation of the principles of justice, equality and mutual benefit in relations among countries and the realization of the right of peoples under alien and colonial domination and foreign occupation to self-determination and independence, as well as respect for national sovereignty and territorial integrity, will promote social progress and development and as a consequence will contribute to the attainment of full equality between men and women."

The preamble of the Convention stresses that "a change in the traditional role of men as well as the role of women in society and in the family is needed to achieve full equality of men and women."

This UN Charter is the result of a unanimous conviction that women's problems do exist. This conviction, however, is not sufficient to clarify the core of the problem and is thus limited to its external form, not to its internal content. For example, discrimination, which is perhaps the most obvious result of this problem, can be attributed to external social factors.

At the time of the charter, UN sociologists were calling for an end to sexism and to the mistaken concept of masculine superiority. In their opinion, the capacity for a woman to bear children does not make her a good mother in terms of society. Similarly, the biological role of the father during conception does not make him a good father in terms of society. Biology is innate; social behaviors are learned.

Presumably, the impetus for the countries who signed the UN charter was to genuinely support women in their march toward equality. However, it seems to me highly improbable that women will be able to attain the position they legitimately deserve unless they can be fully conscious of the deep causes of their own behavior, since their unconscious behavior really does conspire to keep them from achieving self-definition. Is it possible that women themselves make equality difficult and that only when they discover their hidden motivations will they be able to modify the patterns that obstruct self-realization?

The basic concept of this book is: The real origin of women's problems is that women lack their own identities, and lead borrowed lives, made up of elements copied from men. Women live according to male roles because they ignore what it means to be real women, which has different characteristics from what being a man means. Women tend to emphasize biological differences, without giving importance to mental and psychological differences with men.

Amazingly important consequences for a woman's life and for the future of humanity arise from this simple explanation. This book will provide a foundation for this statement. The principle aim of this book is to give women their own identity, so that they will truly know what their psychic sexuality means. They will then be able to be fulfilled through their own expression, not by imitating men.

When a woman returns to her own nature, she has the real possibility to achieve happiness and to rationally build a better world. It is my intent to prove this premise in a strong and rational way. In order to be understood, it is necessary to change the order of certain points in the UN convention. I refer to the paragraph which states that to the degree that peace, international security, disarmament, and mutual cooperation among nations are strengthened, equality between men and women will be achieved. It is my intention to show that the order of points must be reversed, that is, only when real equality between the sexes is achieved will peace be possible.

It is a mistake to try to change external conditions in the hope of solving problems that belong to the inner world of human beings. Only when individuals change internally can they favorably and decisively influence the social evolution of humanity.

To seek equality through a protectionist system will not lead to real equality between the sexes. In fact, to protect implies acknowledging inferiority of the protégé. Along these lines then, it is a mistake to ascribe the problems that women face entirely to the discrimination they experience from men and from the law, which are really related to the external part of the problem. One of the most important elements related to this subject is that, by copying male patterns, the one who imitates will always be irrevocably condemned to a position of inferiority and dependence with respect to the imitated model.

Since women stand to benefit the most, it is important that they become conscious of the fact that equality cannot be achieved through a decree but that it is an achievement that requires individual work, effort, and responsibility.

# INITIAL REFLECTIONS

For the purposes of this book, a survey was conducted by a task force in Santiago, Chile. One hundred and thirty (130) women from various social and economic backgrounds participated in the study. Even though the survey was conducted in Chile, I feel certain that results would not differ too radically from country to country despite cultural differences because people are very similar in their unconscious minds and in their deepest structure.

The women were asked the following questions:

1. What do you believe is the highest aspiration or goal that a woman can achieve in her life?
2. What do you think are the main differences between men and women?
3. Who do you think is better prepared to be happy, a woman of twenty-five, or a woman of fifty?
4. How do you think a woman feels as she approaches old age?
5. What words do you associate with femininity?
6. What fantasies or emotions arise in you when you think of your uterus?
7. Do you think that the uterus could have a use other than for gestating and developing a human embryo? Give reasons for your answer.
8. Would you have preferred to have been a man, or are you content with being a woman?
9. How do you define the characteristics of the ideal man?
10. What do you believe is the biggest obstacle for a woman in her search for happiness and harmony in the relationship with her partner?
11. Can you define the behavior and characteristics of a very feminine woman?
12. Is there a woman you admire as a female role model from the past or from the present?

13. Can you name a woman whom you consider is a disgrace to the female sex? Why?
14. In your opinion, what is the worst defect a woman can have?
15. In your opinion, what do you believe a woman's role is in today's world?
16. What is the worst defect that men have?
17. In your opinion, how do you think a woman likes to be treated in the relationship with her partner?
18. What is the reason women give for having children?
19. In your opinion, who has a greater chance of being happy in life, a man or a woman?

The main object of this survey was to determine whether women have a clearly defined idea about what femininity really means, differentiating it from masculinity, and to find out for once whether women truly understand the main characteristics of their gender. The author also wanted to know as much as possible what their life goals were, as well as their scale of values.

Even though it came as no surprise, the majority of differences between men and women that the women in the survey described referred almost exclusively to biological differences such as physical strength, aspects of the body, and manners. For the most part, the women in the survey ignored characteristics that refer to their psyches, to their internal worlds, and to what type of women they are in their feminine essence. Instead, the majority of the women based their condition of being a woman on the capacity to become a mother. Thus, her role seems to be defined exclusively on the strength of becoming a mother which in turn makes women even more dependent on men. In fact, the first trend to surface in reference to women's problems is their excessive psychic dependence on men. It would seem that women lack not only identity, but also personal goals that are independent from the activities of or the existence of men.

It is well known that the main goal of most women consists of *catching* a man. This goal carries too much weight because when a woman is not able to catch a man she will feel that her life has been an absolute failure. Just consider the different connotations given to the words *spinster* and *bachelor*. A spinster is looked upon as a woman who has failed or as someone who has not been able to become a real woman, stigmatizing her with an image of sexual inability. On the other hand, a bachelor is considered benevolently as an astute person who *did not take the bait*. This means that a woman's existence is not considered independently from the existence of a man. However, men follow their own paths in life which do not depend on women yet do not exclude them either. Women, nonetheless, tend to limit themselves by following in the footsteps of men, imitating their behavior. This is generally how competition with men starts—as an unconscious need to surpass them in some way. This is a futile exercise since it is impossible to surpass the very person one imitates. Thus, both sexes are based on a unique model which is the masculine one: Women revolve around men and not around their own "I." On the other hand, most men do not revolve around women but pursue their own goals. The psychic center of gravity for a woman who behaves as just described is not her own being but rather that of a man.

What are the reasons for such enormous dependence?

Why do women not have identities and destinies separate from those of men?

In order to answer these questions, one would do well to first analyze the genitalia of both sexes and compare them in order to determine the way in which sexuality affects men and women.

Firstly, from early childhood, boys have proof of their sex—the penis is visible and tangible. Girls, on the other hand, appear to have been castrated—not only do they not have a penis but their genitals are invisible since the uterus and the vagina are cavities. Compared to the penis, a girl's genitals are seen in terms of *an absence of*....The result of this contrast is the castration and penis envy complexes. Undoubtedly, this situation definitively conditions female behavior.

According to Karen Horney, a pioneer in the field of feminine psychology, it is probable that the beginning of penis envy first appears as a desire to urinate like men do, especially since little boys seem to enjoy exaggerating the process of urination in a somewhat narcissistic fashion. Little boys have fantasies of omnipotence and a strong urethral erotic sensation when they release a stream of urine. This creates the feeling of being disadvantaged in girls who cannot experience the same erotic sensation as if a pleasure were being denied them. Karen Horney quotes a patient whose desire to urinate like a man occupied much of her personal history to a degree that on one occasion she said spontaneously, *"If I could only ask fate one favor, it would be to urinate like a man, just once, because then I would know how I'm really made."*

The lack of a penis leads some girls to blame their mothers for an abnormality that they believe has made them incomplete. This is why, emotionally speaking, a girl might pull away from her mother and center all of her interest on her father, feeding on fantasies of being able to obtain a penis or a child from him. At the same time, these feelings are accompanied by feelings of hostility and rivalry toward the mother.

The basic points of concern are:

- Men have visible and tangible genitals (the penis). Men are therefore certain of their virility; that is to say, they can depend on it. Men can exhibit their genitals and boast about their penis' prominence which is a symbol of their virility.

- Women do not have a penis. When they compare themselves to men, they feel castrated and develop penis envy as a result. Women cannot exhibit their sexuality through their genitals in the same way as men do externally with their penises other than in the form of a symbolic reference.

Reflecting on what has been said, it is understood that men enjoy a continuous tactile and visual proof of their genitals; therefore, their sexual role seems to be perfectly defined from childhood. Women, on the other hand, have an invisible and intangible sexuality that, at least in infancy, could make them seem like a castrated boy. This experience is reinforced by the fact that, contrary to men, women cannot externally detect their genitals. Therefore, while the penis stands as defiant and obvious evidence of virility, the uterus remains hidden and is valued negatively as if it were just an empty space. In general, with few exceptions, men feel perfectly male whereas women cannot sustain adequate proof of their female condition.

Many women seem to be dissatisfied with their condition and would have preferred to have been born a man. In terms of what is being discussed here it is understandable.

It is important to remember that time does not exist in the unconscious and that the past is experienced as the present. Therefore, one can understand that at such depths the majority of women feel like castrated men and have profound penis envy, intense rivalry, animosity toward their mothers, and oedipal fixation related to their fathers. Since a person's feelings and a large part of one's thinking process are controlled by one's unconscious, women who are not clearly aware might feel like undefined beings that are inferior to males—a kind of man *sans* penis, that is, a castrated man.

This is the way that the feminine sex is born and lives, carrying the stigma of punishment, of subservience, of inferiority, and of dependence. These feelings are accompanied by a profound and floating existential anguish. She compares and associates the penis with power and the uterus with weakness and castration from the depths of her mind.

The anguish that comes from self-devaluation makes women believe that they only have one option available to prove and reaffirm their femininity: *motherhood*. This is how a woman's role comes to be defined solely as that of being a mother which represents to her proof that she is a woman. Demystifying motherhood is not a pleasant task because motherhood is often viewed as a divine command by which a woman renounces her personal expectations in order to form new life. Could the indescribable happiness that expectant or new mothers say they experience simply be the pleasure of having *temporarily* self-defined themselves? The entire drama is hidden within the word "temporarily," because after the birth of the child, once the novelty has worn off, so does the validation of the mother's femininity. It is extremely interesting that psychoanalysis relates being pregnant and having a baby to having a penis in that the baby is the substitute for it.

Why does having a child not mean the same thing for a man as for a woman? Because men do not have to prove something nor prove that they have not been castrated. For a woman, pregnancy is equivalent to what it means for a man to have a penis since throughout pregnancy a woman feels complete and achieves independence from men. Even though she lacks a penis which belongs exclusively to men, during pregnancy she carries out a process that only women are capable of doing and which men cannot.

During pregnancy, the sensation of castration disappears as the pregnant woman is now empowered with something that has an equivalent symbolic value to that of a penis. Unfortunately, the illusion only lasts for the duration of the pregnancy. It is only during pregnancy that the baby is part of the woman, in the same way as the penis is part of a man. After giving birth, the baby goes on to have a separate existence, making it difficult to maintain the feeling of being complete that came from the unification of mother and child in one body. This is why the magic of motherhood disappears so rapidly and is substituted with the obligation of having to take care of the baby. What might at first be an entertaining game soon becomes a duty and the woman feels as empty as before. This is why so many women need to compulsively repeat the experience of pregnancy in order to feel complete.

Since the sexual role of women is associated with motherhood, a woman's entire existence revolves around a man, forever dependant, and expectant, seeking out the *right one* to fertilize her. Whereas men fulfill themselves in life by themselves, women do so through men, seemingly lacking their own values.

What happens to women who do not follow the path of motherhood? They resort to imitating masculine roles and to competing with men. Both options, be it motherhood or the imitation of masculine roles, are unconscious attempts to have a penis in order to overcome the anguish felt because of a lack of definition and feelings of inferiority.

The penis is therefore, both physically and metaphysically, an externalization, a projection or flowering of a virile capacity. Men can be exhibitionists in order to demonstrate their masculinity. This is why they develop external values based on the cult of muscles, strength, agility or the exhibition of academic or financial trophies. The male is an irradiating force that externalizes internal values by projecting them toward the outside. Thus, masculine behavior can be defined as *irradiating, free, and dynamic.*

When women copy men, they are also developing external values, but in order to hide their *deficiency.* The sole drive behind a woman projecting external values is to compensate for her feelings of inferiority and to attract a man, not to fulfill herself.

Female activity thus revolves around the unconscious impulse of catching a man in order to fulfill the role of motherhood.

# A WOMAN'S WORLD

To understand a woman's behavior, it is useful to analyze how women go about their daily existence and to understand their main interests, concerns, and activities. This is the only logical way to verify how women's behavior is based on external values. Underneath such behavior lies a feeling of disdain or rejection of one's own femininity and the reason for adopting masculine roles.

Nothing reflects women's interests more eloquently than women's magazines. Apart from a few exceptions, most women's magazines deal with the following topics: the home, cooking, body beautification, interior decoration, diets for losing weight, tips for staying thin, exercises for keeping in shape, how to fight cellulite, anti-wrinkle products, the latest fashions in order to be more attractive, childcare, the latest love affairs, scandals, and adventures of movie stars and members of the jet set. This makes it seem that a woman's entire life is spent in the middle of beauty creams, clothing, makeup, diets, and a thousand different ways on how to appear more attractive. Such focus reduces and limits the world in which the feminine existence unfolds. It would seem that there is nothing more important in the world than being attractive and having children and one's entire life as a woman is focused on everything external, with emphasis on how to improve one's body not one's mind or one's internal world. What drives this extraordinary phenomenon? What amazing force can oblige armies of women to descend on stores to buy clothes and products aimed at becoming more beautiful, attractive or at having a glowing complexion and lovely figure? More than half the population uses up an important part of their day engaged in such activities. This extravagant waste of vitality is due only to the desire to attract a man in order to be impregnated, to fulfill the role of motherhood and satisfy female narcissism.

A woman's arsenal for being attractive includes beauty, youth, makeup, and wardrobe, and is aimed at raising her self-esteem and getting a man of her own.

Unfortunately, such behavior becomes a hellish trap. Sooner or later, she herself is caught—baited by her own strategy which has already been defined in this book. *Women want to catch a man to get pregnant and to fulfill the role of motherhood in order to overcome castration anxiety in a manner that does not imitate male values. This is the only way for them to obtain a controllable penis.* Women's lives are centered on men. Women develop external values that specifically focus on physical beauty such as reaching and maintaining an acceptable level of personal attractiveness in order to be able to attract a man. Women feel obliged to limit their world because of this focus on external goals.

Therefore, a woman's first wrinkles can be viewed as a terrible threat because with the diminishment of her physical attractiveness she feels the anguish of remaining castrated forever. If her sense of fulfillment depends on a man then her life will lose all meaning when she feels that her power to attract and firmly secure a man wanes or is lost. This also seriously perturbs the mechanism to satisfy her narcissism.

When a woman buys a beautiful new dress or new makeup or gets a different hairdo she can ostensibly raise her self-esteem, causing her depression or anguish to disappear because for a moment she will feel renewed, attractive, and different—more able to achieve her main purpose of catching a man. This makes it clear why a compliment, a daring look or some flattering words have a disproportionately stimulating and euphoric influence on a woman because they give proof to the fact that she still has what it takes to attract a man.

It is clear that under these circumstances women lose any possibility for self-realization as they will only value themselves through men's opinion of them, not through their own.

Logically, it is a huge mistake for women to try to obtain equality through decree because all they really need to do is to place themselves on the same level as men with regard to development and growth of the values true to their own gender. If women would stop copying models that do not belong to them and dedicate themselves to the cultivation of essentially feminine values, they would, undoubtedly, place themselves on equal footing with men since their self-realization would absolutely be of equal importance.

The difficulty resides in not wanting to renounce the role of defenseless adolescent which has been taught to women since childhood as a tool for procuring male protection.

It is important to understand that *equality* not only means the same rights but also the same obligations, and this is impossible in a world of protectors and *protected.* To be sure, the legal rights of women are not being questioned here. Simply, one must recognize the fact that to become of age, one needs to assume new and substantial responsibilities.

The women's liberation movement need not attempt to achieve new and expanded rights without an equivalent increase in responsibilities because, otherwise, this would jeopardize women's authentic liberation. Freedom means to be adult, not adopted protectionism. Women cannot be a kind of creature adopted by a paternalistic society. Instead, they must become adults and be completely responsible and mature. However, women continuously demand more rights and greater protection while, at the same time, like naïve adolescents, they get themselves "adopted" by a man who will take charge of their lives.

While discrimination against women has always existed, it is also true that women in general have voluntarily refused to grow up and develop, remaining subordinated to men by choice. This might be due to the fact that dependency does not require great effort, responsibility or hard work. All that is required is good will to satisfy the protector and to thrive in his shadow.

I am concerned that many women might feel unjustly attacked by some of the concepts expounded upon in this book, erroneously believing that I am making unfair comparisons to men. In truth, the motivation for this book is totally different. My aim is to teach women how to free themselves from their *self-imposed* shackles. Some are so used to the chains that they do not wish to be separated from them.

I would like to be able to expose these matters in a realistic way, not necessarily to be liked by everyone. It is therefore not necessary for me to paint things as rosy, but rather to describe concrete and objective situations that can be proven. So, it is essential to stop believing in fairytales that promise easy and comfortable changes.

All upward transformation requires a great deal of effort sustainable over time. The beginning moments of changing old, mistaken, and useless norms of behavior into others that are of superior quality and purpose are often marked by great anguish. People fear change because no matter how favorable the changes are, adapting to them requires effort. That explains why some people prefer to remain in situations that are tremendously harmful simply because they are familiar, since to make changes to more beneficial situations—even if unfamiliar or unknown—requires work.

I am convinced that women fear their liberation as much as they desire it and that, in their hearts, many of them reject what they so ardently affirm with words. To be responsible for oneself in a situation of complete equality with men can be very frightening. But, the decision to be responsible for oneself is essential for putting an end to discrimination.

It is possible to explain much about feminine behavior that would otherwise not be able to be clarified by women's eternal dependence on men. It can be understood, for example, why the abandonment by a lover represents such a terrible event. From the moment that a man becomes the psychic anchor in a woman's life, the loss of that man is the equivalent to the loss of her own existence. As many men do not understand this phenomenon, they can be too hard on the woman faced with her depression and emotional displays because they do not realize that the loss of affection may make her feel as if she were dying or dead.

A women's magazine is a good indicator of the thoughts that occupy a woman's time. In a local paper, the following appeared:

"THE NIGHT OF THE BLONDE GYPSIES"

"Amid music, dances, and gypsy fortune telling, three pretty sisters, all models, with long blond hair and luminous eyes appeared in gypsy style: 'Dreamy Eyes, Blush and Fiery Lips.'"

Some photographs show various models dressed like gypsies. Their eyes are highlighted by Eyeliner X that makes the eyes seem bigger and the eyebrows thicker and more natural. Product X is said to give the eyes a golden and shiny light, which, as it melts with dark blue, produces an intense emerald color. The blush is a base of orange ochre with a lighter colored blush on top to cast light.

The article continues:

"At night, a spectacular combination of two shades, brilliant silver with mother of pearl and a hue of green result in a smoky sapphire look. The shadows are extended to the temples to enlarge the eyes, etc. ..."

Another article in the same magazine is about losing weight:

"Lose weight with Product Y. It is elegant and easy to use.

"Get rid of excess belly weight by trimming your waistline. Product Y promotes weight loss. It eliminates cellulite. It will modify your body's overall appearance, and so on."

On another page in the same magazine, there is a set of photographs showing the latest fashion in bathing suits. The models are posing like naïve/perverse teenagers biting huge earrings as if they were licking ice-cream with femme fatale expressions and with their hands on their hips in provocative poses.

In another section, a well-known international model is being interviewed. She is a member of the jet set. Lying on the floor, dressed like a Houri, she exclaims, "What I most like to spend money on is clothes. Take this belt, for example, which I bought in Morocco."

The magazine also has a page dedicated to the "BEST GUIDE TO BEAUTY," with pointers on how to lose those extra unwanted pounds, what to do about cellulite, choosing between calories and diets, supplements for losing weight, the value of exercise and sports, and the usefulness of massage as regard weight loss.

Flipping page to page, there are hair-care tips, perfume ads with adolescent girls cooing like babies, horoscopes, and relationship tips—how to keep your man, and so on. Even though there have been many changes in women's magazines, especially for the older woman, the above examples are still true today. Take the latest online magazine website which boasts sections such as: Sex & Love, Style & Beauty, Hot Guys, Celebs & Gossip, You, You, You, Fun & Games, etc.

What am I trying to prove by referencing this material?

The amazing display of frivolous and vain examples is a faithful reflection of the main interests of many amongst the female gender. They do not reveal any profound thoughts or complicated formulas. Everything has to be comfortable and easy to digest. There are no references to authentic feminine values or the development of a woman's internal world.

Everything is based on the external which is essentially designed for cultivating physical charm to attract a man, to prepare for motherhood, or to learn how to become a good housewife.

Is the purpose to catch a man and to be able to keep him? If so, of utmost importance is what a woman whose sole purpose is to catch a man just does not grasp: How to catch herself and become a self-realized, authentic woman.

It is really sad to see how social and cultural patterns have imprisoned women. It is not hard to understand why men do not take women seriously insofar as looking at them as equals when they constantly refuse to have a truly serious existence and restrict themselves to playing games. Women play at living, at marriage, at love, at work, and at fighting for their feminine liberation. In reality, they do not take anything really seriously because they are used to focusing all of their expectations on men. Does this mean that a woman does not need to study medicine to be a doctor; all she needs to do is marry one? The same situations occur in other areas of human activity.

Many women dedicate their best efforts, time, fantasies, and feelings, to cultivating their personal appearance in order to find the right man so they can psychically anchor themselves to him and feel safe. This is why so many women live their lives overly preoccupied with love and everything it entails and are interested in the developing love stories of their friends, acquaintances, movies stars, and pop stars. This is their way to determine how successful or inefficient other women are in finding and holding on to a man. In reality, women are always studying how to intensify their power of attraction, and as a result they do not have any leftover time or interest to dedicate to the cultivation of internal values or self-realization as autonomous individuals. Women are extraordinarily attracted to famous romances because they identify with the heroine and play out the seduction to a certain extent in their imagination.

Of course, there are exceptions to the behavior we have pointed out—mainly among women who need to work to help maintain the family and who physically do not fit the norm regarding attractiveness. However, the differences in behavior are not that profound and are basically because of limitations of time or shortness of charm, and for these women their free time is also spent on some of the above-mentioned activities.

Women, who because of their work cannot concern themselves with these trivial matters, often feel disappointed with their destiny, unhappy, and unfeminine.

Men, on the other hand, due to their social obligations have to confront very serious problems and tough responsibilities and in order to be successful they are forced to center themselves in what they do. Contrast this to what has been stated prior—a woman's main goal is to psychically and emotionally anchor herself to a man in order to be able to live through him.

It is imperative that women understand that they do not need to ask men for permission to become emancipated from them and achieve equality. All a woman needs is to reach psychological autonomy and develop her own potential. Women do not need to appropriate men's attributes because their own are equally important and valuable even if they do not use them. To use feminine qualities, women must learn to free themselves from the chains of frivolity and triviality and from the social and cultural conditions that have trapped them. In fact, because discrimination still exists by which women are considered inferior and less intelligent, it is ironic that in order to keep women passive like babies, society has given them a variety of toys to play with so that they will not bother the adults!

A good example of this is evident in advertising campaigns. Women are used like objects to say all kinds of silly things and to promote the consumption of various products. It is doubtful that advertising campaigns would put the same words in men's mouths if part of a man's role was to wash clothes, having them say something intelligent instead. But as women are considered frivolous and superficial, they are placed in like-minded situations.

The concept of an object woman stems from the fact that women are considered, whether consciously or unconsciously, to be empty or lacking content. This idea is so widespread that she has been stereotyped in the women that appear in soap operas, comedy shows and movies, such as the ditsy secretary who is usually presented as a well-endowed female but with absolutely no brains at all. In reality, this should come as no surprise, as we have become immune by our exposure to models that have a dazzling appearance but atrophied brains. Unfortunately, these are the women most desired by men. And women in turn, try to emulate the success of these models and start to dress and act in the same way. Through this process, day-by-day, women become less of a person and more of an object. In fact, as objects, they have no obligation to grow as persons, just to remain attractive in appearance.

What is the difference between a person and an object?

An object only has an external life and is nothing more than a thing. A person, in order to really be one, must show signs of an internal life. This concept is the precise intention of this book, since it represents the labor women must carry out on themselves in order to become individual persons; women who have turned themselves into objects, have no conscious internal life and seek to borrow from men to live psychically through them.

This is not to say that men are much more adult than women, but to their credit, the male role has not varied throughout the course of history.

Equality must be achieved person by person, by men and by women. It is impossible to achieve equality in a relationship consisting of subject and object.

# FEMININE IDENTITY

Psychological studies about feminine identity have revealed how women have lost the ability to be a person in and of themselves and instead have an identity through someone else. A woman is first "the daughter of," then "the wife of," and later on, "the mother of," which means that she is only *real* when validated by someone else.

Social and cultural factors that determine women's roles are related to historical changes that have taken place, such as the switch from the extended family in the rural and artisan societies to the small modern family of industrialized societies.

In the past, many generations of these extended families lived and worked together for the common good. Men as well as women worked in the home. Men specialized in farming and the women in producing homemade products, thus fulfilling a very important and necessary economic role. Women spun wool, wove cloth, sewed clothes, cooked and prepared food, helped cultivate the land, took care of the animals, and raised children.

Throughout the industrial revolution, the population concentrated in urban areas and displaced the home as a unit of production. This led to the employment of individuals and not of whole families. The production of consumer goods began to take place outside of the home and the only work considered real was the type of work that produced goods or services made for others in exchange for money. Since then, reproduction and the work done at home by women have been considered to be of no economic importance.

On the other hand, technological and scientific advances helped make housework easier, which left women with more free time, leaving them practically unemployed. As a result, the woman lost her status, so to speak, becoming just a housewife, an occupation which was undervalued, offered little satisfaction and created a great deal of frustration.

A defining characteristic of housework is that it does not lead to anything permanent or productive; it is a cycle that repeats itself daily for an indefinite period of time. Women do not receive any wages for their efforts. This prevents them from appreciating their contribution to society. Women's economic dependence leaves them feeling humiliated and neglected.

Due to the lack of a stable internal "I," the role of women has continually been transformed according to historical changes. As previously stated, the effects of industrialization dramatically influenced women's lives, leaving them weak, defenseless, devalued, and disoriented, without knowing what to grab onto in order to find themselves.

On the other hand, the option of motherhood has always existed as a possibility of feminine realization. Currently, because of the prestige and social idealization associated with motherhood, women can feel feminine and complete. Nevertheless, even the role of motherhood revolves around men, since women depend on men in order to be able to realize it. Even the role of motherhood has changed throughout history. Many observable changes have taken place regarding how good mothers should carry out their functions, which will be discussed later on.

For the time being, it is sufficient to understand that the current role of motherhood is perfectly well defined and results in much social prestige. Could it really be true that this is the only role that women are destined to carry out? That is why it is necessary to determine what other possibilities women have in life. This reveals one of the greatest problems for women since no matter where in the world or in which society they find themselves, they seem obliged to assume a subordinated position with regard to men, which certainly must leave them feeling tremendously frustrated.

Steven Goldberg's book, *The Inevitability of Patriarchy*, published by William Morrow and Company, is useful for analyzing certain key concepts of this conflict even though it was published in 1973. Goldberg states that inevitably men hold positions of greater prestige and social importance and they are more capable of being leaders because they have greater levels of aggression. This shows how all societies give greater importance to masculine roles than to feminine ones because, in this way, men obtain the most important roles and positions, thereby fulfilling the most coveted tasks in society regardless of the rights granted to women.

Male chauvinists would be tempted to argue that this happens because women are inferior to men, whereas, the women's liberation movement would say that the real reason lies in the fact that women are socially conditioned since childhood to remain subordinated to men and do not adequately develop their capacities.

Goldberg, however, states that these differences do not correspond to a deliberate intent to leave women in an inferior position, but are based on differences in biological composition. In his view, women are neither inferior nor superior to men; they are simply different, but this difference permits patriarchy to exist.

What does this disparity involve? First, male hormones give men a probable advantage that permits them to better handle social situations in which aggressive behavior leads to success. Male hormones make men more aggressive, or make them have a lower threshold before releasing aggression. Consequently, men are better able to acquire roles and positions of greater importance. Young boys are socially conditioned to attain roles of command and prestige.

Goldberg goes on to say that "hormones make social behavior inevitable. The higher the level of power, authority, status, prestige, or position, the greater the percentage of men, be it in politics, economics, professional, or religious arenas." He also points out that patriarchy is a universal fact because in spite of the great variety of political, economic, religious, and social systems, there has never been a society where authority and leadership have not been in the hands of men.

He also emphasizes the phenomena of male domination, which is an emotional sensation felt by men or women by which the will of women is somewhat subordinated to that of men, and how the overall authority in mutual and family relationships falls on men.

This is how, biologically speaking, from the start men could be assured of a dominant position within any historical or institutional framework, while women would retain the exclusive capacity for motherhood and the feminine power to convince men to be able to get what they want.

Analyzing all of the above, we may immediately understand why women feel discriminated against by men, ardently demanding greater access to positions of prestige and power that have nothing to do with motherhood. On the way, many women succumb to the temptation of competing with men to obtain positions they desire. However, most women are likely to become frustrated if they try to reach the highest positions and most important roles they seek because their lesser capacity for aggression puts them at a disadvantage when they come up against highly aggressive men.

Although some women may succeed, they very often do so at the expense of losing their femininity. This implies that their success is because they have faithfully copied male roles and become strongly aggressive and competitive, which in turn can negatively influence the hormonal system and make one more virile. This could result in abnormal deepening of the voice, growth of hair, a desire to command

and dominate, and the adoption of masculine attitudes. This is the price of success. Therefore, by renouncing femininity, such women reach the level they were seeking. This is not a triumph for women, but for men. One only needs to observe women who stand out as leaders in politics or any type of leadership over the masses.

Where is the woman who is able to maintain perfect femininity while holding a position of power?

In sum, it would seem, therefore, that the female sex only has three possibilities with regard to fulfillment in life:

1. To conform or give in to a subordinate role
2. Motherhood
3. To compete with men for positions of power and prestige

Bearing in mind that penis envy and the castration complex make women feel undervalued as they perceive that they lack a part of the anatomy that men possess, one is able to understand that these sensations are dramatically confirmed in the material sense. Men seem to succeed in areas where women are not able to and therefore seem a lot more fortunate or superior. Not only do they have a penis, but, apparently, by having one they also have a set of favorable circumstances that speak for themselves: they enjoy greater freedom and less social repression; they are not subject to the pain or discomforts of pregnancy; due to the nature of their sexuality alone, they occupy important positions of authority; and, above all, they dominate the most highly valued and important social roles. That is why motherhood inevitably seems to be the only field in which the female sex possesses absolute exclusivity and superiority.

It would seem that Nature has obliged women to be mothers or to conform to subordinate positions at men's sides. Under such unfavorable circumstances, it is no wonder that women imitate male roles. Unconsciously and as if by magic, women are convinced that they can become equal to men by copying them.

The consequences of this are quite obvious. Women imitate male roles in the hopes of obtaining the same success by copying a winning model, yet at the same time, they do everything possible to extol erotic attractiveness to the maximum. Consequently, their identity is tied up with being a mere female, not a feminine person. By seeking femininity through becoming a coveted erotic object, development as a person is not possible.

A great majority of women therefore associate femininity with erotic objectification. In seeking to become more feminine, they use things that emphasize their sexuality on the outside, but not on the inside, in the conviction that such elements make them "more of a woman": clothes, makeup, hairstyles, and adornments for enhancing their erotic object status. Such women do not stop to think that such adornments are not necessarily accompanied by internal definition. The end result is women who dress up as women but who internally copy masculine roles.

How can one describe the model of the modern woman?

She is genitally defined as a female. She dresses in accordance with current fashion and social trends; her makeup follows the dictates of fashion; and, externally, she might appear to be the typical woman representing the dominant stereotype, but she does not possess internally either definition or personal development. In fact, once the choice of becoming an erotic object has been made, she castrates herself as a woman. The first aspect of a woman's sense of castration has to do with her sense of incompleteness because she does not have a penis, either feeling mutilated or created incompletely. The second aspect seems to almost indicate voluntary castration because she moves away from her feminine nature when she tries to recover her wounded self-esteem by focusing all her possibilities on her physical appearance and becoming an erotic symbol. The ongoing search for self-validation through external things (beauty, youth, makeup, clothes), has the unique purpose of attracting a man, not searching for self-realization.

Carlos Castillo del Pino, a well-known academic and psychiatrist, wrote many in-depth essays on women. He said that the common condition of women in society has to do with their peculiar type of alienation. He commented that the most profound type of alienation in women is accompanied by a loss of awareness about their own alienation. To be a member of the female sex implies a handicap. In reality, women are objects to men and are used by them. Women are erotic objects for men. Del Pino says that for women, the fight for life has been modified into the fight for a man.

He wrote about the woman's frustration that she must go through in learning her function. What are the various stages of this frustration? The main point of the evolution of female frustration seems to be the assimilation of passiveness, from the special consideration she receives at an early age—which implies weakness when compared to boys—to the greater delicacy in the way she dresses and the decidedly different nature of her games and activities. It is obvious that even she can verify the difference in her training compared to the training that men go through. Furthermore, from early on women are constantly reminded that they are defenseless and need protection—from men of all people. Del Pino adds that it is not necessary for girls to feel the lack of a penis in order to experience the castration complex. It is sufficient for them to experience the full range of influences that have previously been alluded to that push them towards passiveness and dependence. Traditionally, in all societies of the world, men are expected to be strong and aggressive and women passive, sweet and selfless.

Cultural patterns of humanity established passiveness as a fundamental condition of femininity. Aristotle justified paternal and marital authority by stating, *"The authority of men is legitimate because it is based on the natural inequality that exists between human beings."*

Even during Aristotle's time then, women were devalued from the metaphysical point of view because they were thought to incarnate the negative principle of matter, whereas men were thought to personify form— a divine principle synonymous with thought and intelligence. It was believed that women carried out a secondary function, and similar to the earth that needs to be fertilized, their only merit resided in being a good womb.

In her book, *Mother Love: Myth and Reality,* Elisabeth Badinter refers to the stigma given to the female sex by Christian theology. She alludes to the words of Genesis on the creation of man and the circumstances surrounding original sin. First of all, it is supposed that God created man, but when he saw that man was disappointed because he lacked a companion, God supposedly induced him to fall asleep in order to remove one of his ribs and create a woman from it. Therefore, woman was born from man.

The moment in time when woman appears as the responsible party for sin and the subsequent downfall of man is an important milestone. The serpent promised Eve that she would be similar to God and would know Good from Evil. Once Adam had fallen, God apparently recognized woman's guilt and imposed the following anathema upon her: "I will greatly multiply thy sorrow and thy conception"; "In sorrow thou shalt bring forth children"; and, "Thy passion shall be to your husband and he shall rule over thee."

According to Badinter, the concept of passion implies passivity, submission, and alienation, which would come to define the future feminine condition. After being confirmed as the dominant one, Adam was condemned to merely work hard and die like Eve.

Badinter states that from this story, a whole series of consequences for the image and condition of Eve emerge. She is more vulnerable to temptations of the flesh and vanity; her weaknesses make her guilty for man's fall from grace. In the best of cases, she appears as a weak and frivolous creature. Later on, she was likened to the snake itself—a devil temptress—and she became the symbol of evil.

In her book, Badinter cites Count Benedetti (of the late 1800's) who said that when a woman denies obedience to her husband, she is opposing God's commandment. God wants women to submit to the rule of their husbands, as men are more noble and excellent than women because they are made in the image of God and women are only made in the image of man. Benedetti also insisted on the evilness of women. In fact, at that time it was quite common to refer to women as *she-devils*. Slowly, however, this reproach was transformed and was softened into a concept of weakness and female worthlessness. This concept of a wife obeying her husband was included in the French Civil Code at the time.

Many great thinkers in history, like Rousseau for example, have maintained that a woman was not made for herself, but rather, she was made to please a man, to be subjugated by him in order to be pleasing to him, to give in to him, and even to tolerate his injustices.

In sum, a woman's psyche reveals the following points:

- She is repudiated and punished by God himself, who has sentenced her to be subjugated to a man. This carries with it a tremendous stigma, which is impossible to erase and will follow her forever.

- The lack of a penis makes her feel diminished and induces her to develop a strong feeling of inferiority, which compounds her penis envy.

- A woman's hormonal system triggers less aggressiveness than men's. A woman tolerates a higher level before releasing aggression. This diminishes her possibilities of success with regard to attaining roles of command and prestige.

- A woman is socially conditioned to assume maternal and passive roles, preventing her from participating in activities in which men predominate. Since childhood, she has been indirectly told that "due to her weak condition she must not do this, that, or the other," activities that are instead done by men, for which they are rewarded.

- A woman's maternal role condemns her to passiveness and suffering since she must give birth with pain and be responsible for educating and bringing up the children. Thus her possibilities for education and independent work are limited or restricted.

- A woman becomes an erotic object when she concentrates all her possibilities for progress in life on trying to catch a man.
- Finally, as an erotic object, a woman does not fulfill herself sexually. This can be verified by the large percentage of women who are frustrated, unbalanced, frigid, or dissatisfied.

These points also explain the lack of contribution from women to science, culture, inventions, and art in earlier centuries.

It is no wonder, therefore, that women develop considerable existential anguish, much more than men, and try to distinguish themselves and excel even if only by imitating men.

However, women are not right to blame men exclusively for their discrimination because, according to Steven Goldberg, sociologist and author known for his books on patriarchy, males and females are socialized or mentally influenced to fulfill their own possibilities in the best way they can, based on the biological characteristics of each sex. In this way, if a girl is socialized to be repressed and discouraged from activities that require aggression, strength, command, or dominance, she is simply being freed from experiencing inevitable frustration in the future because she will never be able to attain the highest levels in these roles. In this way, society arbitrates the means to administer the available natural resources, which would permit reaching greater efficiency and strength. In reality, we must recognize different characteristics in both sexes.

Following this line of thought, it is not possible for women to rebel against divine authority, deny their lack of penis, alter their hormonal system, or fight society for having mentally influenced them in this way. In reality women are left only with the option of motherhood or copying male roles in order to be able to enjoy that which men enjoy, risking in return their own femininity.

Are women then inevitably and irrevocably condemned to be subordinated to men? According to Goldberg, yes, because males have always been and will always be dominant in any type of society due to inalterable physiological structures that have been modeled by evolution and handed down through genetic codes.

For my part, without completely discarding some of the aforementioned arguments, I believe that women can achieve complete and absolute equality with men, not through legal decree but through their own realization. Self-realization must integrate a desire and determination to do so, as well as a perfect understanding of the psychological and social mechanisms that keep women subjugated. To take effect, this will obviously require a massive coming together of women who are committed to this purpose. The path to achieving this purpose will be touched on in later chapters.

At the risk of redundancy, it must be repeated that such a resolution must be born from a profound understanding of the mechanisms that impede the feminine sex from finding her own identity and from having access to her own self-realization.

# DIFFERENCES BETWEEN THE SEXES

For women to stop imitating male roles there is a need to understand the principle differences between men and women. The first order of the day is to find the causes behind a woman's regular behavior to determine when her behavior is masculine or feminine. To be able to find out what qualities are intrinsically feminine we must unravel tangled emotional states, attitudes, norms of behavior, anger, envy, hatred, jealousy, and frustration. Only then will it be possible to understand how to possess truly feminine qualities.

As stated in the last chapter, women do not know what femininity really is. In search of this precious quality, women tend to confuse it with physical beauty or the experience of motherhood. The lack of psychological definition that has frustrated her throughout her whole life provokes feelings of inferiority, neediness, and weakness.

In a comparison of a group of men with a group of women, the following characteristics were observed about the group of women:

- A greater amount of anxiety or existential anguish was manifested as a predisposition to emotional hypersensitivity and neurosis
- Greater dissatisfaction with life
- Greater group uniformity with greater personal rivalry
- They came together as a group of women, and not as feminine individuals

In contrast, men are less predisposed to neurosis, dissatisfaction, bitterness, and frustration, even though they have been known to go mad and commit suicide more frequently. When men get together, unspecific rivalry is not present other than rivalry that stems from concrete and objective reasons. They do not unite as a group of men, but as individual persons tightly united with common interests.

What is the root of female dissatisfaction?

Undoubtedly, a woman's dissatisfaction stems from the perception of her anatomical lacking, from a feeling of inferiority in comparison to men, from the certainty of having fewer privileges than males do, and the knowledge that men hold authority and prestige because they created culture and civilization.

Not only dissatisfaction exists in women, but also a profound anger and envy toward the male sex because, traditionally, men have occupied preferential positions in all aspects of life. In some ways, men are perceived similarly to how a slave sees his master.

Generally speaking, men find relative balance between work, marriage, children, and recreational activities. Women are more often obsessively polarized on certain things that they convert into psychic fixations. Physical appearance, social recognition, the home, the all-absorbing frenzy of finding *the ideal man*, are maniacal goals that seriously perturb a woman's emotional balance and, at the same time, stop her from seeking out other areas of greater interest and importance with regard to her own development.

Women have a latent insecurity that makes them feel constantly questioned and on trial. In fact, it seems that a woman must constantly be proving things. She needs to prove that she can be a good wife, a good mother, that she is the perfect choice for carrying out certain tasks and that she is sufficiently responsible. In reality society does not consider her an adult, but an infantile being that needs to prove she has grown up sufficiently to deserve certain things. Regarding this point, it is important to note the different connotations conferred on men and women regarding the failure of a marriage or love affair. If a man fails in marriage, he is seldom questioned or put on trial. He simply writes it off as a normal event. It is a totally different matter for a woman. She is not considered adult or sufficiently mature, developed, able, or ideal. Her failure in marriage leaves a very different scar since she often ends up being shunned socially.

In reality, regardless of the angle from which this is viewed, women seem to be measured by a very different yardstick than the one used for men, and circumstantial appearances do not seem to favor her at all. When a woman is young she anxiously looks for a goal with which to define herself. When she gets married and does not work, she feels like a prisoner overwhelmed by housework. If she is married and works she feels anguished and divided because she has one foot at home and the other at work. If she has no children she might feel frustrated. When she has children and the novelty has worn off she feels the anguish of having sacrificed her personal expectations.

Throughout her life and after menopause, a woman feels that her possibilities in life have been exhausted beyond repair. She has nothing left but to wait. If she has a companion she is always aware that she might lose him. If she does not have one, loneliness makes her feel abandoned, defeated, and undervalued. It appears therefore that the life of a woman is much more difficult than that of a man.

A woman's sexual development is a lot more complex and difficult since she must make two important changes that men do not need to make:

1. Change of the love-object, (transfer the love she has for the mother to the father)
2. Change her erogenous zone (transfer sensitivity from the clitoris to the vagina)

Men do not need to make these changes; their love object will always be feminine and they also possess one erogenous center—the penis. Since they have a penis, they do not need to prove anything. The achievement test that society asks from women really means: *Show us that without a penis you are able to behave correctly, because until then, you are on trial.*

Many circumstances tend to reduce women to nothing and place them in a position of inferiority and subordination. In the last chapter, there was reference to theological repudiation, the lack of penis, a lesser amount of aggression released by the hormonal system, socialization toward motherhood and passivity, being treated as an erotic object, and disturbing feelings about orgasm. In addition to this list, there are some additional obvious disadvantages that are a consequence of a woman's lesser muscular strength, a lesser capacity for the abstract, and a precarious emotional balance.

Women, on the other hand, are less affected by hypertension and cardiovascular diseases. Fetal mortality is higher among boys than girls and the number of spontaneous abortions of boys is higher throughout pregnancy. A greater percentage of males die within the first month of their lives, but more males are conceived than females. Furthermore, a woman's immune system is more efficient than that of a man.

Other biological differences follow:

- Men have less genetic information because the Y chromosome is the result of the X chromosome minus an arm. This extra arm is in all female cells and is known as Barr chromatin, an indisputable sign of the cellular sex.

- The embryo becomes a girl when the primary sex cells populate the mass path of the ovarian cortex. The same embryo would become a boy if the nucleus were not populated.

- This previous fact describes the root behavior of the sexes, which in a woman takes the form of welcoming, internalizing, enveloping, possessing, receiving, and nurturing. In a man, the form is irradiating, free, and dynamic.

- The temperature of the female body is 0.4-0.6 degrees higher than a man's regardless of where the temperature is taken.

- Girls are born with and experience their first menstruation due to their female hormones; men have no contact with their hormonal system until they are seven years old.

- Whereas men have a gonad stability that is only weakly influenced by the seasons of the year (probably due to the amount of light), women are periodically alternating between a fourteen-to-twenty-two-day cycle of estrogen and another fixed fourteen-day cycle of progesterone.

- The amount of red corpuscles in a man is 2 percent higher than in a woman.

- Male hormones are produced in women in the nucleus of the suprarenal glands. Female hormones are predominantly produced by men in the ganglion near the lumbar aortic vertebrae.

- With respect to the pituitary gland, development of the anterior part is normal for men. For women, development of the posterior part is normal. This is where anti-diuretic hormones are produced as well as oxcytocine and a precursor of prolactine. In men there is only one anti-diuretic hormone.

- The average weight of a female human heart is 9 ounces and a male's heart is 10.5 ounces.

- The female liver weighs 49.4 ounces; the male liver weighs 56.45 ounces.

- The third ventricle in men is larger than in women and probably contracts more quickly as a result.

In his book, *The Natural History of the Mind,* author Gordon Rattray Taylor gives some examples of physiological differences between men and women.

Firstly, some physiological differences between the sexes, many of them from birth, may affect cognitive styles. Girls have stronger senses of touch and taste; they are also bothered by loud noises. They are more skillful than boys and possess better night vision. Boys react more quickly, feel the cold more, and are distracted a lot more by new things than are girls. Little girls show a greater interest in sounds immediately after birth, and therefore, this might be inherited.

Secondly, women have a higher activation level; they get excited more quickly than men. This was tested with an EKG. Women seem to feel more affected than men by alarming or urgent situations.

A third observation dealt with left-handed children who hold their pencils in an upright manner (there are those who hold them like a hook). Left-handed children's brains are, for the most part, lateralized in the opposite direction to the norm, meaning that the verbal center is on the right side. (The term *brain lateralization* refers to the fact that the two halves of the human brain are *not* exactly alike.) In this group, results studied by the author revealed that girls were better than the boys at spatial tasks and the boys were better than the girls in verbal tasks.

The author cites evidence that boys are more lateralized than girls. This might explain why it is easier for men than women to handle a machine and speak at the same time because they use a different hemisphere for each function. Women are better at actions that cannot be separated in this way, since they coordinate speech and movement with some difficulty. The lack of hemispheric specialization in women may be the strange explanation why women are twice as likely to confuse right from left as males! If lateralization can explain some sexual differences, then it would be greatly important with regard to hormonal functioning, especially those hormones that relate to sex. Male and female hormones are different from the time they are in utero. Hormones influence conduct and physical development, including the development of the brain. Cognitive style is affected by hormones. Female hormones reduce the level of a group of inhibiting substances called monoamine oxidase (MAO). People who have lower levels of MAO are much more easily excitable.

Taylor cites Paula Johnson and Jacqueline Goodman who said that women tend more than men do to solve problems by using their weakness and asking for help. This is a rather well-known occurrence and does not require further studies. It is fairly accurate to state that a woman with a flat tire will usually convince the first man to come along to change it for her. But it is more difficult to determine whether this behavior is due to actual physical weakness or to an old habit of solving problems through men because women are physically weaker.

In order to continue to try and solve the enigma of the behavior of women, the aforementioned characteristics can be linked to debatable discoveries made by Havelock Ellis. Ellis strove to scientifically establish which traits depend on the female constitution and are therefore biologically determined and which ones are because of fashion, habit, education, or superstition. He defined three important female traits determined by biology:

1. Greater affectability compensated by a greater invulnerability
2. Lesser tendency towards variation, that is to say, less apt to produce genius or degeneration
3. Biological conservatism and childishness which has to do with the direction of the process of evolution

Ellis pointed out that women's organisms are more highly affected by oscillations and stimuli of smaller degree. On the other hand they have a greater resistance to more serious perturbations. Said differently, women are strongly affected by small incidents but adapt more easily and resist far better when faced with great catastrophes that destroy men. "Her affectability is counterbalanced by her greater invulnerability. The characteristics of her vasomotor system contribute to this, since it is less stable and responds more quickly to stimuli, which makes women much more impressionable, irritable, or open to suggestion." Ellis notes that due to a thinner consistency of a woman's blood, a higher level of anemia, and periodic excessive excretion of calcium during menstruation (calcium compounds have a great influence in vasomotor stability), a woman is subject to increased affectability and neuromuscular weakness.

These biological characteristics translate into psychological behavior—the interaction, reinforcement, or inhibition of behavior that starts with behaviors already examined. In the example of women having contributed far less to culture than men, their behavior could be due to their lesser tendency toward variation than men; that they possess a more concrete type of thought than men; that it is more difficult for them to think abstractly; that women are socially conditioned for motherhood and to carry out passive roles; and that women also have an organic tendency toward stability and conservatism.

Furthermore, femininity has traditionally been associated with passivity and masculinity with activity. Freud derived characteristics of non-movement and passivity from the egg and activity and movement from the sperm. If one takes into consideration that women have less psychic energy than men because they use up a substantial amount of this energy trying to realize their sexual evolution, which is much more complex than that of men, we will understand that this development process uses up so much energy that a woman's level of sublimation is inferior to men. Due to this, women tend to be more focused on specific personal problems and less interested than men in social and cultural events.

On this matter Freud says that women are not simply indifferent to culture but have a hostile attitude toward it. This is because men, faced with the many demands posed by their role, must also carry out tasks by distributing their psychic energy in a proportional manner. This implies that the time and effort spent on cultural matters is taken from the time a man would spend with his wife and family. Therefore, his spouse might feel she is put in second place because of the demands of his cultural activity. In turn, in such a case a woman would have an adverse attitude towards knowledge. Because the whole opus of civilization is a male creation women do not want to have too much to do with it. Women also perceive that it is not an area where they can easily excel.

On the other hand, Karen Horney and others explain the predominance of men vis-à-vis cultural contribution as men's "envy of motherhood." According to Horney, as men realize the small part they play in creating live beings, all their efforts become directed toward cultural productivity as a way of compensating for their uterus envy. Curiously, a similar phenomenon that in women leads to such negative repercussions—penis envy, feelings of inferiority, etc.—in men, uterus envy drives them to creativity and self-realization.

If women are subject then to greater affectability, they will be much more dependant and vulnerable because of their hormonal system. A drop in estrogen levels might bring on negative feelings with regard to self-worth as well as anxiety, depression, and irritability. Estrogen levels fall regularly before menstruation, just prior to giving birth, and during menopause. Menopause coincides with the appearance of several psychological and psychosomatic symptoms—extreme emotional sensibility, outbursts of tears, depression, disorientation, confusion, lack of concentration, irritability, headaches, dizziness, and flashes. Sometimes women become intolerant, anxious, and hypochondriacs. High levels of estrogen correspond to positive mental attitudes, as low levels do with negative emotions. Men are not affected by a similar phenomenon because the decrease in testosterone takes place very slowly and gradually. The precariousness of women's psychic and biological balance is confirmed by these responses, despite the fact that women are stronger than men when it comes to dealing with major upheavals.

Theodore Reik, a prominent psychoanalyst and student of Freud, theorized that people who were made physically ungracious or handicapped by nature often behave as if they were owed some kind of compensation or special treatment, as do women who lack a penis. Due to a belief that nature deprived women of the coveted masculine genitalia and accorded them a disadvantaged position because they were born women, the world, in women's unconscious thought, is divided into "those who have" and "those who have not." The conviction that men owe them and must pay arises from this belief.

With regard to men, women feel greatly ambivalent. On the one hand, they admire men, and on the other hand, they despise and envy them. This explains how women internalize male values and fight against them at the same time, despising their own femininity all along.

Because of the anger and envy women feel toward men, they pervert their passive condition —a principle female characteristic—by taking advantage of their weakness in order to collect from men what they are supposedly owed by them. Their apparent weakness is exploited to dominate and control men, so that they will be protected by men who are to continue to compensate them for their weakness. This attitude automatically kills a woman's own possibilities for development.

Two well-defined options for women surface: either they fight against being women, renounce their femininity and imitate masculine roles, or they pervert their passive condition and use it as a weapon to dominate, manage, and control.

Men and women act very differently with regard to success and happiness. Men are continuously driven to expand and push toward reaching for their goals. They may succeed or fail, but they are constantly striving for self-fulfillment, and their psychic energy is constantly flowing toward achieving their goals.

Women, on the other hand, experience this very differently. A dominant trend in their lives is passiveness and frustration. Their disillusion starts with genital inferiority and is reinforced throughout their education, which is much more repressive than that of men. From the beginning women are filled with the notion of being weak and needing protection. In turn, a woman's options in life—both internally and externally—are considerably decreased when compared to those of men because of this accepted concept. The limited opportunities are projected internally as if they were inevitable. As soon as a woman resigns herself to this, she will conform to those functions that were deemed essentially feminine by tradition and social definition—becoming a mother and homemaker.

A woman's personality is also influenced by the repression of certain erotic impulses that flow much more freely in men. One of the most important differences has to do with female narcissism which is quite different from that of men. In fact, narcissism in men takes on the form of a mechanism employed to highlight or simulate their own worth as it pertains to masculinity, while narcissism in women has to do with a fixation and arrest at a childish oral level, which naturally translates into immaturity. That is why femininity is identified with childishness and beauty which diminishes over the years, when in reality, the opposite should happen. This misconception comes from an absolute lack of knowledge about femininity, mistakenly basing it on high levels of estrogen.

Infantile fixations represent a serious obstacle for individual maturity while, on the other hand, they offer certain advantages that have to do with guidelines that normally rule erotic attraction. The child-woman, no matter how immature she may be, increases her erotic value in the eyes of men because of the belief that a woman's erotic value becomes irrelevant as she loses her youthfulness. This belief implies that women become desexualized as they age and that there are only two kinds of women: girls and matrons. Girls are identified with greater femininity and matrons are identified more in terms of being a human being than being a woman.

This drives women to paint themselves in as infantile a manner as possible—both externally and internally—in order to maintain their quality of an erotic object.

Female narcissism is a mechanism of self-elevation and self-appreciation as an erotic object. Therefore, one could declare that women's primary goal is to appear as an erotic object in order to fulfill the basic objective of catching a man.

Unfortunately, this mechanism is a hellish trap that works in the following way:

- A woman's primary objective in life is to find and hold onto a man.
- She turns herself into erotic bait in order to fulfill her primary objective.
- She is forced to perpetuate the child-woman state.

- A direct consequence of the above is to continue being a child and be castrated as a woman in the sense of becoming a real, full-grown, adult woman.

By analyzing this behavior, one can see that women spend enormous amounts of psychic energy on matters that have nothing to do with self-realization. Strength that should be used in their own development is lost and, by not fully using their faculties, women end up destroying or castrating themselves.

If one wants to raise a woman's status in order to eliminate discrimination and allow her to occupy an equal place next to men it is important to accept that this can only be done through individual development. She must be encouraged to abandon the child-woman role, the erotic-object condition, and be offered alternatives for not being obliged to imitate masculine roles. Instead, she needs to develop and fulfill real femininity as an individual, mature, and adult person.

It is essential to face this problem in its real dimension, so that women do not deceive themselves with the mirage of freedom that is legally instituted. No external law can substitute for a fully developed, feminine "I." In fact, the more one fights to protect women through decree, the more one encourages their weakness and helplessness because they will continue to be recognized as being so helpless that society is almost obliged to take care of their existence. One must, once and for all, recognize the undeniable fact that a woman's emancipation really means emancipation from herself—freedom from her mechanisms, norms, and behaviors that sustain her total alienation.

No decree, state referendum, or international organization can foster a woman's individual development. All they can do is defend a woman's equal rights with regard to men within a legal framework. This is the same as what would happen if half of humanity was small and laws were passed to protect their rights instead of to stimulate their growth.

The basic problem resides in the fact that women have spent so much time frustrated and limited that they have gotten used to their so-called weakness and inferiority, and instead of growing up psychologically, most prefer to remain small in order to exploit this weakness and obtain protection.

It is important to repeat that emancipation for a woman is in reality freedom from herself. It involves severing the harnesses of the patterns that keep her alienated from her true feminine nature.

Returning to the issue of feminine narcissism and its consequent draining of psychic energy, it is important to observe that women do not put on makeup or beautify themselves only for one man. Once married, they extend their projection as erotic bait to all men. Since a married woman already has a husband one might assume that she would not want to catch another man, and it becomes clear that her objective is erotic self-appreciation.

The ongoing search for admiration is not aimed at finding a man, but it does satisfy her narcissism. This is obvious since women look at each other much more than they look at men. In fact, there is a type of flirtatiousness among women, nothing homosexual about it but based on the constant need to feed one's ego. When this happens, external beautification is aimed at impressing and calling the attention of other women. This is easily observed in the attitudes of two women who meet on the street, or in the behavior of friends or acquaintances who have just met. They observe each other from head to toe faster than the speed of sound and with an expert eye in order to evaluate the value of the so-called rival as an erotic object. This is, in reality, a type of female stock exchange. The value of a woman's own stocks must be checked daily. Understanding this will help one to penetrate the mystery of a woman's world of makeup, hairstyles, and clothing to which men actually pay little attention other than as a sort of frame.

What is the point of fixing one's hair and makeup so carefully if men do not really notice all the details? The answer is simple: women beautify themselves for other women, not for men. In fact, mostly it is useless to ask a man's opinion about which dress or hairstyle works best because they will tend to show little interest in the question or even avoid answering it completely.

Reik stated that there are only two types of men who show genuine interest in women's dress: homosexuals and fetishists—the former because they unconsciously want to be women and the latter because they are seeking a penis on the female body to counterattack an unconscious fear of castration. In this way, the object that becomes the fetish symbolizes a penis. Through this unconscious imaginary mechanism, fetishists manage to fight their fear of castration that becomes tremendously strong when they see a naked woman.

Were it somehow possible to capture, capitalize on, and direct the psychic energy of human beings, a large quantity of energy deployed to maintain female narcissism would be enough to take care of all the needs of humanity! Think about the force that is activated by crowds of women who tirelessly shop, go to beauty parlors, and work out in the gym in order to increase their level of personal attraction and thus raise their level of erotic narcissistic satisfaction.

Del Pino, who was cited earlier, says that narcissism, specifically in women, in order to be constantly gratified, demands constant training of it, undivided concentration, the impossibility of distraction and the employment of all of a woman's physical and psychic resources. Anyone trained to observe totally narcissistic personalities is aware of a very serious fact: the endless resources needed in order to obtain more and more gratification. Narcissism is like a bottomless pit. When can narcissism truly be satisfied? The answer is "never." A narcissistic personality gets insecure the moment its needs stop being gratified. There always exists the threat that the gratifying object switches its aim elsewhere. The narcissistic personality needs constant feedback and constant gratification and seeks it insistently by adopting new attitudes in order to maintain the level of required gratification

Female vanity is a reaction stemming from the conviction that one is at a disadvantage. Accordingly, dress for example, is a way to compensate for this lacking through apparent beauty. According to Reik, clothes are a psychic extension of a woman's body and when a woman says, "I have nothing to wear," she is really saying from her unconscious, "I have no penis." Women sometimes use pants as a way of identifying with masculine roles. Perhaps the wearing of pants by women was first adopted to feel safer emotionally speaking by identifying with men, using an article of clothing that had traditionally been male. Clothes have a tendency to become sexualized and the word skirt has come to mean "woman" and pants have come to mean "man." In this way, she can temporarily forget the anguish of castration. In truth, fashion is a parallel phenomenon that does not mean that the mechanisms are any less real. Fashion, as with many social customs, is not accidental but is generally motivated by unconscious factors.

# MISTAKEN BEHAVIOR

It is essential that women open their eyes to the real motives behind their actions. Only in this way can a woman become responsible for herself. As long as she feels she has the right to blame a man or society for her problems she will not look within and will continue to justify her conflicts and difficulties. When a woman does not assume responsibility for her actions she perpetuates the condition of self-alienation. This alienation originates in part from within her and in part from socialization. Self-deceit is a common human practice used to avoid facing frightening realities. This mechanism results in a progressive separation from reality that can cause a person to live in a world of absolute fantasy.

When women live through *unconscious* behavior, it impedes their individual development. This is what is referred to as *mistaken behavior*. It is extremely important to know about these mechanical ways of being, the symptoms of which are easy to observe.

## PASSIONATE BEHAVIOR

Women typically display more passionate behavior than do men, such as excessive enthusiasm, impulsiveness, euphoria, explosiveness, and sentimentality whether it is positive or negative. It is precisely this passionate behavior that makes women susceptible to self-deceit. Because this leads to self-alienation, women become more attached to their imagination and fantasies, confusing reality with their own daydreams. It is not surprising that as a consequence of this alienation, women tend to commit quite lightly to matters that will later lead them to experience great emotional damage, sometimes even material loss.

These characteristics correspond to the female traits of irritability and affectability described by Ellis. These mechanisms can lead to nervous and emotional imbalance. The balance of a woman's emotions and feelings is precarious. It is as easy for a woman to have fits of anger, aggression, or rage, as it is to have feelings of kindness and maternal love.

Unfortunately, in society women who are passionate are considered more feminine, when in reality the exact opposite is true, especially if one's goal is to consider women as persons and not simply as females or erotic objects.

Passion stems from *passiveness* indicating a passive feeling, not an active one. In this state the woman-person is alienated, while her erotic component dominates her behavior. Unfortunately, the most pernicious consequence of this impassioned state is the lack of selectivity in reference to alienating stimuli which entrap her. By responding only to external influences, she becomes obliged to act in a specific way and cannot escape its domination. When a woman is confronted with reality, which is imminently active and vital yet absolutely unpredictable and indiscriminate in the way it manifests, her heightened emotions overflow her usual brain paths, and it becomes impossible for her to maintain self-control or think rationally in those moments. The more connected a woman is to her impassioned behavior, the less of a person she is because a passive woman becomes a passive object.

Real femininity must be based on the ability to discern objectively. This capacity is not innate; it can only be the result of individual development and depends on an internal decision and willpower motivated by a completely comprehensive understanding of the feminine condition.

It is unlikely that persons with a low scale of values will make the effort to seek self-realization and comprehend how far they are from individual maturity because maturity presupposes taking responsibility for one's own existence. However, when one sees oneself truthfully, at the beginning it can be a blow to one's self esteem and it is important to remain positive. This is why it is difficult to start this work because people often idealize themselves, believing they possess an innumerable amount of qualities and virtues that in reality they do not have. Since it is hard to become an authentic adult and human being, people deceive themselves under the guise of acting as if they had already achieved this. Unfortunately, maturity is often associated with external behavior such as drinking alcohol, smoking cigarettes, the use of foul language and lax manners, a compulsive lack of inhibition, and over-eagerness to live intensely through physical pleasure. These are some of the modes of behavior that are usually copied to appear mature.

Those who think that common sense comes with age as a natural result of the passing of time make a terrible mistake. It is only possible to become an authentic adult through a profound and sustained personal effort and few are able to achieve it.

Similarly, becoming a real woman has nothing to do with age, hormones, passion, or physical appearance. It has to do with an individual realization based mainly on the cultivation and development of inner values.

There are many reasons why women become passionate. Some of the principle reasons are due to jealousy, pride, vanity, spite, wounded self-pride, feelings of being humiliated or disdained, envy, defensiveness, and resentment against men. This excessive sensibility is not only part of women's classic emotionality, but springs from strong feelings of inferiority felt from an early age due to the lack of external genitals.

When a person feels questioned, that person might become hypersensitive to criticism, giving excessive importance to approval from others. This latent insecurity generates aggression and an exaggerated need to defend oneself, which in turn predetermines nervous and emotional instability. In the end it translates into a difficulty to control oneself, in other words: passionate behavior.

To a certain degree, this volatility of character is what makes many men not take women seriously, using the argument that women are not reliable because they change their opinions all the time and hardly ever keep true to their word or stick to their original purpose.

Obviously, when a person is prone to emotional fits or exaltations, that individual will constantly change his or her mind. Unfortunately, life's circumstances make it more likely for a woman to get hot tempered and lose control rather than stay calm and in command. The passionate route is a downhill slide, whereas self-control and higher rationality require a sustained effort in an upward direction.

A husband or partner who has tried many times without success to make his wife or partner understand his point of view through elaborate rational explanations might in reality be experiencing some of the consequences of the behavior referred to here. Whereas a man's conviction usually comes from logic, a woman's conviction is often based on an emotional obsession that excludes all other possibilities. This recurring stubbornness does not usually last long nor is it very consistent. In fact, it may do a 180-degree turn from one day to the next, leaving in its wake a sort of confusion, lack of consciousness and/or disorientation due to the shift in position that has just occurred.

## UNHEALTHY COMPETITION

Compulsive competitiveness is a fixed component of female behavior. On the one hand, women compete with men to compensate for their overwhelming feelings of inferiority, and on the other hand, they hide a latent and quiet rivalry with other women. While men can usually live together in perfect harmony even in large groups, subject only to differences based on very specific reasons, women, behaving as females, cannot sustain harmonious and calm relationships even within small groups of friends because there is always a pending rivalry and aggression that does not exist among men.

Even though women may appear to be good friends, taunting, sarcastic or hurtful comments lie just under the surface, waiting to come out.

What is the origin of this peculiar style of relationship?

What is the reason for this continuous antagonism? The reason is very simple indeed: it is due to fierce competition to catch a man. Men might compete because of various activities related to their professions, but women compete because of one main activity: catching a man, either to convert him into her eternal companion or to keep her narcissistic mechanisms alive.

While, as was stated, male rivalry is most usually professional in nature, women seem to have only one profession—to be attractive to men. This full-time job induces them to compete among each other. This behavior in women covers a profound anguish since it seems as if their individual destiny depends exclusively on success in this endeavor.

Men and women have completely different perspectives when it comes to the subject of loneliness. For men, loneliness represents a lack of affection and human company. For women, it represents a kind of psychological death and a life without hope. The reason for this is based on a woman's anxious search for a man. She believes she will be able to do through him what she does not feel capable of doing alone because her sexual role is so undervalued. Logically, since she cannot become a man, having one to identify with becomes a viable option.

The biggest mistake a woman can make is to strive to become dependent on a man because she will never find a man who is reliable enough for her to be able to hand her existence over to. The delicate and complex nature of human communication makes it almost impossible for people to understand and accept what others specifically expect from them. Furthermore, there is often also a conflict of interest. A woman may feel deceived by a man who has not fulfilled her expectations without stopping to consider that he probably does not even know what her expectations are, and that she had never established these requirements as a prerequisite for their relationship.

It is normal for individual expectations to be different. That is why a woman should not demand that a man give up his own points of view to satisfy hers.

Women need to understand that to depend on men for their own happiness and well-being is both irrational and illusory because these states can only be achieved through a steadfast adherence to one's internal world.

Is it realistic to believe that a being exists that is strong and perfect enough to be able to carry the weight of an additional life on his shoulders? To wait for a man to make one happy is nothing more than the attitude of an object that passively waits to be provided with joy.

One of the ways that aggression manifests in women is through certain characteristics of language. When a woman talks with a forked tongue, she is using one of the most terrible weapons available, engaging in her own cold war. Reik referred to this condition as viper-like and gave some examples of double-talk among women that only they understand.

Reik stated that women can be quite vicious when they talk among themselves in the presence of a man who may not be in the least bit aware of what is going on. He may hear what one woman says to another and understand the words, but not the hidden meaning. However, the women are not speaking in a secret language. The words used are taken from everyday language and from everyday conversations. Yet they have a double meaning that only another woman can understand, just like in a suspenseful espionage story. The longer a man takes to realize it, the greater his surprise. For example, a man goes out to dinner with his wife. At dinner they meet one of his wife's girlfriends, who says to his wife, "Anne, you know I always liked the way that dress looks on you." The husband has no idea that the compliment is really a criticism.

He quotes other examples along the same lines, recounting the story of when, some time ago, he had been sitting next to a young lady at a dinner. An older lady passed by the table where he was sitting and said with a kind smile to the young lady: "You look so pretty this evening Muriel, I almost didn't recognize you." This is another example of criticism disguised as a compliment.

Another example is taken from a conversation Reik overheard between two women in a university cafeteria:

First woman:     "Tell me, what do you think of Jane?"
Second woman:  "Jane is a nice girl."
First woman:     "Oh! I'm so glad that you don't like her either."

This aggression comes out almost naturally because all women can be seen as dangerous rivals who will stop a woman from catching a man or holding onto him. It is worth noting that nowadays such rivalry is at its highest point ever in our history. The reason for this is due to certain scientific advances and to greater female liberalism. The result is that there are considerably more available women. This is true not only with respect to the marriage market but also to the flirting market, which stimulates narcissism. In fact, plastic surgery and developments in the cosmetic industry have created situations where mature women appear to be much younger than they really are. Thus, women who were not able to compete in the past, can now do so quite successfully because they have rejuvenated their erotic attraction. Similarly, young adolescents, wearing makeup like adult women, compete side-by-side with their elders.

It is important to remember that according to the guidelines established for erotic objects, what really matters is personal appearance. So, women are actually victims of their own traps. The search for recognition as erotic objects has increased the number of available "females." The general complaint that women have currently is that they do not know where all the men have gone or that there simply are no men.

While the ratio of men to woman has stayed more or less the same, by broadening the ray of male erotic interests, there are in fact more women for the same amount of men. This creates the illusion that there are not enough men. It is understandable that this generates a considerable amount of anguish as women feel the stress of being single. This in turn can make a woman hysterical or neurotic and break down in her weakest point. Even married women are not free from this worry. Since now she not only needs to be attractive for her man, but she also needs to continue attracting other men in order to feed from the narcissistic reaction that this admiration brings her.

## *FRIVOLOUS ATTITUDE*

The Superior "I" is able to internalize certain values that can considerably assist a person who is reaching for important goals. The formation of the Superior "I" is more difficult for women because women do not have the same need as men to overcome the Oedipus complex. (The Superior "I" is created thanks to the repression of this complex.) Since women do not fear castration as men do, they are not driven by fear, as men are, to overcome it.

As a consequence, women tend to stay in the same situation for an indefinite period of time, leaving it behind only late in life and most often, not even completely. As a result, her Superior "I" does not have the strength and independence necessary for achieving cultural importance and, therefore, her social interests are much weaker. Her impulse toward sublimation is also rather limited. Both these important restrictions limit her to a certain degree regarding participation in cultural and creative activities.

From another point of view, for several centuries many women have also felt a type of repulsion toward culture, which had become a kind of symbolic lover for her partner, if there was one. If not, it was still perceived as a potential threat. A possible explanation for this repulsion or fear is explained by the fact that the more their men participated in cultural activities, the less time they had to dedicate to their wives or partners and families. The woman therefore cultivated profound aversion toward these interests.

Furthermore, many women do not feel a great desire to participate in the evolution of the world since they view its structure as something that is clearly masculine. Therefore, to participate in its evolution seems like a thing for men and not for women. Also, women are socialized since childhood to fit into the maternal role and avoid everything that requires sustained and intense effort or abstract thought.

Throughout their education women are not encouraged to develop creative thinking, but rather to cultivate primarily erotic attractive qualities and to adapt to the desires of men.

Instead of being encouraged to develop intellectually, women have been told that men do not like intelligent women, and that men do not appreciate a woman's knowledge, preferring instead a more passive woman, a pleasing, sweet, soft, maternal, affectionate, and selfless woman. No explanation is given why she cannot be all those things at the same time: intelligent, sweet, soft, maternal, and affectionate.

As a woman's intelligence is usually compared with that of men, it is important to remember the theory that suggests that a man's cultural activity is motivated by his envy of motherhood because when he realizes that he has very little to do with the creation of living beings, he tries to compensate through cultural creativity. Naturally, what motivates a woman is not the same.

Women also lack the tendency toward diversification described by Ellis as a masculine impulse that stimulates brilliance.

For a long time, the mandates of society have placed the responsibility of maintaining a family on men's shoulders, and in some ways, allowed the women to be less confronted by such complex, sustained, violent and varied requirements. A man must be strong; he must be responsible; he must not fail; he must not cry or be weak.

This is why women have a greater tendency to behave frivolously and superficially. Simply observe their habitual telephone conversations and informal chit chats. It seems that the more frivolous or trivial the subject of discussion, the greater the sensation of pleasure, freedom and emancipation.

It is important to note that this frivolous or superficial attitude is simply an expression of well-known female insecurity. It is a self-defense tactic that she employs when she believes she is dealing with matters that are too important or incomprehensible, which by contrast make her feel insignificant. Connecting with all that is trivial also underlies her avoidance of responsibility.

Imagine an adolescent girl who unexpectedly finds herself in a conversation with a famous, cultured and intelligent individual. It is understandable that her weapon of choice to hide her possible ignorance or lack of experience would be to behave frivolously. If her frivolous chatter is seen as a manifestation of feminine flirtation skills then, for obvious reasons, it will be turned into a tool to be used at all times with men and with women because it will become her normal way of relating to people. However, this type of childish verbal expression becomes a real obstacle to developing her intelligence because of the positive feedback she receives from flirtatious and frivolous behavior.

Furthermore, if a woman possesses a sharp and well-trained intellect it will not be possible for her to appear weak in order to get a man to protect her since her intellectual strength and the need for protection would contradict each other. By exploiting her passiveness in order to catch a man and have him be her protector, she is limiting herself intellectually because in order to maintain the privilege of being protected she needs to limit her intellectual development. To be able to maintain an image of helplessness she must only talk about frivolous or unimportant matters but she must feign an attitude of disinterested feebleness that for some reason she has associated with the traditional concept of femininity. Unfortunately, this attitude is centuries old and it has mutated into a self-defeating mechanism that restricts personal talent. If an individual, no matter how intelligent, is obliged to appear mentally restricted for an indefinite period of time, that person will end up forgetting how to think and/or their intellect will atrophy.

The dilemma in which the female sex finds itself can become a vicious circle; if a woman continues to identify with being weak and avoids intellectual activity in order to exploit her so-called helplessness and passivity, she will end up castrating herself with regard to her self-realization as a woman. If she opts, on the other hand, for individual development she will have to renounce men in their role of adoptive father and instead take on new and heavy responsibilities.

A difficult choice! History has shown us that so far, women overall have preferred to remain passive.

Could it be then that women's liberation movements merely want to confirm that women are weak, needy and helpless individuals in need of special laws to protect them? Such movements fight to halt male expansionism, but do not encourage the need for women to emancipate themselves from the internal forces that keep them psychologically alienated and prisoners of subjective socialization and misunderstood personal progress. It would seem as though only women are oppressed by the paternalistic society that deliberately wishes to discriminate against them forever. This view does not take into account the fact that they have subordinated themselves by denying themselves a process of authentic individual growth and from assuming responsibility for their own lives. Such women expect everything from society and very little from themselves.

If women had greater access to education and work opportunities, it would not necessarily result in giant steps toward ending discrimination. Evidence proves that women have not made significant development as feminine beings and have only increased their legal rights. Many, who presumably consider themselves emancipated, have adopted masculine roles in order to compete for higher positions. This does not mean that they have freed themselves as women. In fact, many have become mentally and psychologically masculine. Can this be called progress?

Usually, women only perceive too late in life that they have paid a very high price for their supposed independence and emancipation because they had forgone any possibilities to fulfill themselves with respect to their authentic femininity. Authentic femininity is an internal matter that does not depend on material circumstances.

With one foot in the home and the other at work, women are far from feeling satisfied.

## *LIVING FOR APPEARANCES*

Women generally live for external appearances much more than men. They seem to value everything that is apparent, external, and tangible, what they can see and touch, devaluing that which is internal. They prefer physical attractiveness over sensitivity, intelligence, understanding, sweetness, softness, and comprehension. That is why a woman puts all her expectations in her external appearance. That is also why when they start to lose their youthful charms life becomes a drama as fearful and threatening as death itself. I remember a beautiful young actress who told the press, *"I have the feeling that my life will be very short; that is why I must take advantage of what I have now and enjoy every moment to the fullest."* I do not think she was referring to physical death, but to an unconscious intuition that wrinkles would be arriving shortly, prematurely ending her career, which was based on her external beauty and not on talent. To her, the deterioration in the smoothness of her skin and the filling out of her figure signified personal extinction.

Recall that the narcissistic self-gratification mechanism previously discussed needs constant feedback in order to maintain its female vanity. The eagerness to base one's destiny on external appearances and all that it entails is thus easily understandable. Since women are not satisfied to be attractive only, they ardently need to be outstanding in everything that symbolizes an extension of their bodies or personalities. As clothes represent an extension of the body, women need to renew their wardrobe frequently to avoid feeling out of sorts. Makeup and clothing allow women to beautify their physical appearance. Unexciting or outdated clothes make women feel insecure and lower their self-esteem, even if their faces and figures are truly beautiful.

There are some women who deny their femininity and identify much more profoundly with the external masculine role. These women do not take care of their physical appearance (the only thing they consider feminine), renouncing all efforts to make themselves beautiful. So, women go to extremes; they either let everything depend on physical appearance, or they disregard their appearance and start to look masculine.

Many women divide their lives into two well-defined stages. The first one, which is very short, starts with adolescence until the appearance of the first wrinkles. This period, according to a woman's unconscious appreciation, represents her true life as a woman, that is to say, the period in which a woman will be greatly desired by men. The second stage that lasts until physical death is seen as the phase of despair and disappointment. It is the period of resignation, to live like an old woman, waiting for the natural course of events that are supposed to bring a certain amount of material pleasure, but that have nothing to do with feminine self-realization. It is difficult for a woman at this stage to completely feel her femininity because she still might not know what it means, having made femininity a physical component all these years.

Men have a fixed sort of internal sexual identity. For the most part, their gender is not only obvious, physically speaking, but also psychologically. Women, on the other hand, seek their internal identity by projecting outwards, trying to fulfill themselves through external values and seldom through internal values. Under these circumstances, since external conditions are unpredictable and varied and a woman is obliged to continually adapt and identify with new situations, she can lose contact with her fragile internal identity.

In general, men represent the external factor for a woman. She will thus identify quite closely with him and begin to live psychically through him, taking on similar characteristics to the ones he possesses. When she changes companions, she gives up the personality she had temporarily adopted with the previous partner and assumes a new personality according to the new man.

Women do not possess an internal "I" that is fixed and stable. Instead, a woman's "I" is projected outward and is embodied in material situations. Men also do not have a developed, stable, and mature "I," but because of their continuous confrontations with the responsibility, obligations and challenges that life demands from them, a certain something that is intrinsic to their masculine identity has been created internally. This does not imply judgment of worth, but men do have a center of psychic gravity, albeit odd, small, and primitive. Due to this, men can carry out feminine tasks of any kind without becoming feminine. Women, on the other hand, due to their lack of an internal feminine "I," become masculine when carrying out work usually done by men.

When women choose a partner, external factors also come into play in a decisive way. Generally, their selection is based on physical appearance, economic position or the important image that the individual projects onto the world. A man is seldom chosen for his intrinsic content. This is the reason for so many erroneous choices.

Since women externalize their own essence, they become progressively empty until they are reduced to only an image of femininity. This is the predictable result of a life lived frivolously and narcissistically, focused on insignificant details and an extreme preoccupation about one's physical appearance. This preoccupation makes a woman particularly vulnerable to criticism.

Reik maintains that women are always on the defensive in their relationships with men. They blame the man in advance to protect themselves. Reik states that a woman's intolerance or hypersensitivity to criticism is fundamentally due to her fear of losing recognition with the opposite sex. A woman's hypersensitivity with respect to criticism is the result of a lack of confidence in herself. When people feel strong, they can recognize personal mistakes or defects because they are confident about their qualities. When one is on guard, one reflects doubt and uncertainty about one's own virtues.

The female sex knows that men have a great need to idealize them. However, if the ideal has defects, it can no longer be ideal. According to capricious models of divine perfection imagined by imperfect beings, the ideal must appear to be perfect. Women can recognize faults and weaknesses in a man and still love him, but they fear that if their own defects are out in the open, they will no longer be loved.

This provides another strong reason for women to want to maintain appearances at all costs. They need to idealize themselves in the most perfect manner to raise their self-esteem. "Out of sight, out of mind" in this sense means that, as long as a woman can deny her own defects and faults to herself she will be able to falsely simulate her own perfection. At the same time, her main worries might be the following: to wear the latest highly suggestive and provocative fashion and the latest makeup; to have the newest hair color and style, to have good skin, to know the latest Hollywood gossip, to know who is involved with whom, to know which stars and musicians are the most popular, to be up-to-date with TV dramas and soap operas, and so on.

Beauty pageants, because they place so much value on external factors and appearance, illustrate this point perfectly especially since most young women cannot deny that they secretly aspire to be chosen as a beauty queen.

There seems to be a type of hydraulic relationship between people's internal and external parts. By means of various communication vessels, all vital and psychic energy is concentrated wherever the "I" is centered. In this way, inner energy flows towards the outer layers, an act of suicide that in the end leads to the death of the whole system. This is where the main problem of women resides: By only being interested in the outer layers, she forgets that she has a trunk and roots that need to be nourished with life's experiences if she is to grow and develop.

A woman's alienation can be compared to a tree that has been sucked dry by parasitic plants that have extracted her vitality. There is only one difference: Women can free themselves from this plunder if they wish to.

## THE COMPULSIVE DESIRE TO POSSESS A MAN

It is natural for a woman to want a companion, but it is not appropriate for her to avidly want to catch a man merely to compensate for her feelings of inferiority. However, it is obvious that a woman generally looks for a man in order to possess him, as if, with respect to her personal fulfillment, she could not exist independently from him. Men try to fulfill themselves through their work; women tend to do so through a man. To do so, a woman will try to hoard or monopolize a man by controlling him psychologically because she fears that, if she were to lose this opportunity, she might remain without any possibility for fulfillment in life.

Due to the feeling of castration, she does her best to possess a controllable penis in order to satisfy her infantile desire to have a penis and feel complete. When she approaches a man, it is not out of simple love attraction, but with the intent of appropriating for herself—symbolically speaking—his masculine virility. When her appetite is too intense, the woman develops a domineering and possessive personality. The principle object behind such an intensity to possess a man is to ensure that she will have her own male genitalia forever, and overcome her castration anxiety. When a woman feels she can handle a man and keep him under her control, her neurotic anguish calms down. This anxiety originates, as we already know, from her feeling of lacking.

This explains why a woman might feel terrible anguish when she perceives that her companion might escape her control, in which case she would be castrated once again. I believe that the loss of a love is generally experienced by a woman as a new castration, especially when the separation has been decided by the man. When the woman ends a relationship, it is as if she were getting rid of a worthless penis that is just not virile enough.

The expectation of being stripped of the genitals she took possession of in her imagination is a very threatening situation, a source of frustration, and it brings on feelings of inferiority, humiliation, self-pity, and guilt. In fact, if she is stripped of them, she tends to feel that it must have happened as a form of punishment due to a great feeling of guilt, not by mere chance. This is an explanation for how her unconscious translates the experience.

Women discover their castration when, as little girls, they perceive that there are other little girls that have a penis, and there are those, like themselves who have been deprived of one. This happens at an early age before little girls can detect the differences between the sexes. Boys are seen as girls with penises. In their unconscious, according to their primitive and infantile way of thinking, they deduce that they have been castrated as punishment for incest because they felt erotic desires toward their fathers, turning their mothers into their rivals.

Clearly, the unconscious only seeks to avoid problems. It only pays attention to the anguish caused and tries to calm this anguish by taking away the symptoms without considering the real cause of the problem, just like taking a pain killer for a headache.

Possessiveness and the drive to dominate function as a sedative for the woman who has not overcome her Oedipus complex. When a woman dominates a man, her anguish created by the lack of male genitals, calms down. However, as is often the case when the symptom is treated and not the cause, the problem is not solved but it becomes worse or remains latent in an undefined manner.

In the case of the sedative-scenario, women temporarily calm their anguish, but become addicted to the drug and need to consume it constantly. In other words, such a woman needs to keep a man under tight control. There are cases, more than less, where this dosage is not enough, and it becomes necessary for her to increase it until she completely possesses a man's brain, including his emotions and impulses. This unfortunate mechanism creates the exact opposite situation than what was hoped for because when men are driven by their self-preservation instinct they refuse to be absorbed or psychically digested and, without consciously realizing what is happening, they run away with a compulsive determination even if it means losing or curtailing the great love they may have felt for that woman.

Nevertheless, there are other cases of men who can be feminine, passive and timid, and who accept the control and domination. This scenario is even worse for a woman because, by not having an opposite pole to balance her, her virile behavior is reinforced and she ends up becoming completely masculine. Therefore, if a woman succeeds in fulfilling her craving to dominate, she becomes masculine; if she is not able to impose herself, she might feel terribly anguished and castrated.

One of the things that a man fears most from a woman is for her to be domineering and possessive because he instinctively feels that she is the castrator, that she is really trying to castrate him or that she wants to take away his free will with regard to his thought and actions. He perceives that his virility—the force of his creative action—will be annulled if he loses his freedom.

When a woman is domineering, manipulative, and possessive, she is not able to give to her companion or the relationship. She is instead continually demanding. This type of behavior is found in all individuals who have a weak "I," who, in order to compensate for their lack of individual energy, need to rely on external reinforcement. Such individuals feel the anxiety of constantly needing to be admired, flattered, and revered in order to raise their self-esteem.

The consequences of this behavior are quite disconcerting. A woman who is permanently worried about controlling her companion becomes externalized to the maximum and increases her emptiness. She thus loses her chance to live life fully and instead feels a great emptiness. This empty feeling motivates her need to *receive* in order to fill herself somehow. The act of receiving in this case is not healthy or normal, but is instead a sick and limitless desire to absorb. This desire can never be satisfied because it is motivated by the woman's unconscious rejection of the female role and by her obstinate persistence and eagerness to have a penis.

Therefore, the controlling behavior that she uses in order to hold on to a man brings about the opposite result. This situation is not without its drama because such a woman will live with the feeling of being constantly unsatisfied, no matter how much she receives. Nothing will be enough because what she really wants is to have a virile organ.

Freud said that "women never resolve their Oedipus complex because the only solution would be for them to accept castration." This means that a woman needs to give up her unconscious eagerness to have a penis, and that she must accept her feminine condition.

## ANTAGONISM TOWARD THE OPPOSITE SEX

It seems a great majority of women have strong feelings of hostility and antagonism toward the male sex.

This naturally originates with penis envy because it is the mere possession of a penis that seems to coincide with many privileges. In fact, from an early age little girls start to realize that boys have greater possibilities for erotic satisfaction because they can hold their penis when they urinate without being punished for doing so. This is somehow interpreted as permission to masturbate. Girls, on the other hand, have an invisible sexuality and are often severely reprimanded for touching their erogenous zones. Right from the start then, it would seem that boys have access to some kinds of satisfaction that girls are not allowed. Later on, they see, too, that male aggression is encouraged, whereas their own is strongly discouraged and repressed. They also come to realize that they are heavily restricted with regard to freedom of movement, unlike boys who are allowed to move more freely. Later on, they begin to understand what motherhood means and how painful giving birth is and they start to see only the disadvantage of all of these circumstances. They can also see that they are educated to be passive and helpless. Slowly, they realize that there is an abyss between the sexes, one with privileges and the other somewhat reduced.

This feeling of inferiority becomes a source of deep resentment against men. They might feel driven to disqualify men at all cost or to beat them at their own game. Because they envy men, women copy them while all the while remaining internally convinced that they will not be equivalent to the original.

Latent rivalry spurs penis envy in women, inducing them to reject their feminine condition and to assume a decidedly masculine attitude.

This is how the phallic woman came into existence—a sort of psychologically masculine Amazon woman, despite her physical attractiveness. Her psychic virility prohibits her from honest, collaborative relationships with men. It also stops her from being able to truly give of herself wholeheartedly in order to achieve real communication in love. Without realizing it, she assumes the role of the male. She will try to possess a man in order to hold onto him. The phallic woman has not been able to find a balance in her relationship with the opposite sex; she either adapts to a man's desires, thereby relinquishing her individual development and remaining passive, or she stubbornly opposes him.

At times her hostility can be so intense that it bubbles up to the surface and manifests itself as a violent desire to castrate or cripple men. She does so by psychically dominating men or keeping them under her control. This is compounded by the fact that a woman's aggression is a lot more subtle than a man's because the feminine condition has been idealized and that idealization does not permit a woman to lose her reputation, as explained earlier. Her aggression is covert and passive and often takes on the form of rejection concealed as loving concern. She has subtle ways of repudiating her man with feigned tiredness, frequent headaches, migraines, sudden attacks of sleepiness when she feels she is being criticized, and a variety of psychosomatic disorders. These are her tools to show her anger. Frigidity, too, is often due to aggression and the desire for revenge, manifesting so subtly in order to sustain a continuous level of erotic provocation, while at the same time refusing to engage in the sexual act.

Her defiant provocation is usually sustained through a negative passivity, closed obstinacy, hidden rejection, and verbal aggression.

Many young women who truly wish to attract and keep a man are often surprised at their inability to do so. Some may believe the reason is because they are not very attractive. What they do not realize is that they are really strongly ambivalent – both agreeable and adversarial at the same time. They might use hurtful and sarcastic language to point out their dislike for male attitudes that do not satisfy their narcissistic requirements. A man who does not realize what is happening and feels perplexed, bothered or confused, usually prefers to leave.

## CHILDISHNESS

Henry Havelock Ellis, a British doctor, sexual psychologist and social reformer, considered childishness as one of the three main feminine traits. He defined it as the state of a woman who is close to nature, in that it exists to preserve her freshness to benefit possible offspring. He believed that biological conservatism and childishness have to do with the evolutionary process.

However, there are other aspects of childish attitudes that have to do with a lack of individual development, or rather, a fixation at early psychological stages. In fact, female narcissism has to do with becoming fixed at the early oral stage. Another point to consider is how the erotic role becomes less relevant as youthful attributes are lost. Note also the way youth is accentuated in women's fashion. Many models employ childlike poses; they dress as adolescents, biting an earring or licking an ice-cream cone that is popular with young children. This is because youth has been eroticized, while mature sexuality has been neutralized. This phenomenon is also in line with the old female behavior, whether innate or spontaneously adapted, of a woman who wants to be protected by a man. To accomplish this, she needs to pose as a helpless little girl, otherwise it will be almost impossible to awaken the man's protective instinct. In reality, women are cultivated from an early age for this. She is taught that her path is to get married, so she must find a man to take care of her. This is rather obvious in the woman who views marriage as a symbol of liberation. On the other hand, most men see marriage as implying duty and responsibility. In fact, there is a saying in some countries that girls always worry until they marry, whereas boys never worry until they do.

Many young girls are brought up by their parents to believe they are too weak to carry out heavy tasks and that it will be difficult for them to take care of themselves all alone. They are told that this is the reason why they need the protection of a strong, brave, responsible man who is not prone to debilitating sentimentality, who never cries, is immune to fatigue and pain, and who has an unlimited capacity to provide. This man is, in other words, a second father as well as a superman.

Esther Vilar, author of *The Manipulated Man,* states that women become a man's pupil in order to attain their own security. She says that a woman's search for stability goes as far as to use her own children as hostages to hold onto her husband.

It seems that one can only be a pupil if one appears or pretends to be weak, helpless, psychologically and physically immature. Under these conditions it is impossible to have an egalitarian type of relationship, which is an essential requirement to have a mature and happy marriage. Otherwise, there will always be a pseudo father and an adopted daughter, not a real loving couple.

This is the main cause of male infidelity, according to Vilar, since it is impossible for a man to satisfy both the impulse to protect and the sexual instinct with the same woman. As these impulses are irreconcilable, men seek resolution by having more than one woman. When a man has more than one woman, he can continue to protect the adopted daughter, thus fulfilling his impulse to protect, but he can also fulfill his sexual instinct by having another sexual partner.

Thus, because of this system, which has been in place for a very long time, adult women, generally speaking, do not exist, only girl-women who pretend to be small in order to awaken the impulse to protect from men. Among those who could be adults, there are many women who in a way turn into men, becoming more masculine as they imitate male roles.

Women in general spur the system on, whether consciously or unconsciously, by carefully hiding their strength to appear helpless, weak, air-headed, and fragile. In reality, the opposite is true since life as a male entails a handicap from conception until death (more on this subject in the Appendix of this work).

When we compare the sexes, one of the most revealing differences between men and women is how seriously they take their lives. The majority of women are girl-women who take their existence and their lives as a game. They only take things that have to do with their safety seriously. They play at falling in love; they play at working, at having a social life, at being a housewife, at motherhood, at a passion drama, at sewing, and so on. Perhaps, for many women there is no significant difference between playing with dolls as little girls and having a baby to breastfeed. It appears that childhood games never end; in fact, they just go on for an entire lifetime.

Men are shocked to realize that there is very little apparent difference between a ten-year-old girl who is wearing makeup and dressed as an adult and a mature woman. The result is identity-confusion where one cannot clearly define who the girl is and who the woman is.

One of the things that men reproach women for—whether openly or not—is their lack of seriousness with regard to commitments and attitudes, as well as their lack of respect toward solemn, important or transcendental matters. Is it not true that when men and women go to the opera, for example, while the man is paying attention to the music or scene, the woman is paying greater attention to the way other women (her competitors at the same event) are dressed, their makeup and their jewelry? Men are unconsciously aware that nothing seems to be taken seriously, as if life were a rehearsal, a play or even a joke.

Del Pino, the Spanish neurologist and psychiatrist, said in an interview that appeared in a prominent financial magazine that the greatest waste in education is the brain drain of many women who stop their intellectual pursuits to simply carry out their perceived duty and no more. (Their duty refers to taking care of the children and the home.)

Even though studying for a career does not seem like a game, it is understood that these studies are a type of life insurance in case one's marriage fails, and not a defined choice of occupation central to her existence. This means that the seriousness of her commitment varies; it can be pursued or put aside, just like a game.

## SADOMASOCHISM

Helen Deutsch, a disciple of Freud best known for her writings on the "natural masochism" of women, defined women through three main characteristics: passivity, masochism, and narcissism. According to her, boys and girls initially have the same level of aggression, but cannot express it in the same way. Masculine aggression is directed outward and is not usually shunned by society, whereas a girl's aggression is directed inward. This repressed aggression which is turned inward toward the "I," becomes a kind of female masochism. According to Deutsch, women cannot avoid their tendency toward masochism as if it were a necessary condition for passing through the main stages of life: sex, birth, maternity and the various stages of reproduction that are somehow linked to suffering. Based on this understanding, it would seem that women simply fulfill the punishment bestowed on them by the Creator in order to expiate original sin.

Karen Horney stated early on in her career that women sought specific satisfactions through their feminine sexual life and maternity which were masochistic in nature. She said that a girl's early sexual desires and fantasies regarding the father represented a desire to be mutilated, in other words, castrated by him. Even menstruation has the hidden connotation of a masochistic experience. What women secretly desire in sexual commerce is rape and violence, and in the mental aspects, humiliation. Giving birth represents an unconscious masochistic satisfaction. The same occurs in the relationship of a mother with her child. Ms. Horney also stated that when men fantasized or performed masochistic activities, these acts represented an expression of their desire to carry out female roles. She wrote that there is no need to discuss the fact that women may seek and find masochistic satisfaction through masturbation, menstruation, sexual relationships, and giving birth.

The intention of this book is to analyze this behavior in how it harms a woman in her love and emotional life because it tends to be one of the main hurdles blocking the achievement of happiness and personal development.

I believe that the female sex feels more joy than annoyance in being subordinated to men. Women protest strongly against male chauvinism, yet the chauvinists or macho men seem to be so much more successful with women. How else can one explain why women accept abuse for so many years, complaining bitterly, but seemingly happy underneath it all? Could there be a secret pleasure in being raped and humiliated? Some surveys that explore erotic fantasies seem to substantiate this point. Through such imaginative excesses, a woman can have an orgasm that she cannot obtain in any other way.

Suzanne Horer, in her work on the sexuality of women, recounted some fantasies that resulted from a survey of about 13,000 women. These results were then published in a magazine.

"When I am with my husband, in order to reach orgasm much faster, I imagine that I am a prisoner or a slave that is punished and whipped. I imagine that I am prostituting myself like the character in the Story of O, in the scene where she is whipped, to help me become sexually aroused and have an orgasm. I already had this fantasy before I saw the movie." (35, married with children)

"In my fantasies, I am always the woman that is dominated by a man who imposes his will on me. These fantasies started to appear after I read erotic books when I was a young woman between the age of sixteen and twenty. I imagine that I am being sodomized and penetrated by three or four men who do with me what they want, or that a man makes me prostitute myself. In another fantasy, my husband threatens to make me pregnant, and the thought of getting pregnant, turns me on." (Forty-four, married)

"I really love my husband, and he is a good lover, but in order to reach orgasm I need my fantasies. I imagine that I'm a prostitute like in the "Story of O," in an elegant house, where I am sodomized and beaten. I let this happen to me; It hurts me but the orgasm is very good."(Thirty, married with children)

"I am raped, sodomized, and penetrated everywhere by a group of men that have their way with me. Or a man gives me to another; he puts me on a table, lifts my skirt and sodomizes me while the first man watches. In another fantasy, I am the only woman present and am handed over to a mob of men by an older man who orders and supervises my rape or sodomizing." (Forty, married)

It could be argued that these fantasies belong only to sick people, but this would be a mistake. It is important to remember that on the unconscious level there are no moral rules and instincts are expressed freely. It is the Superior "I" that represses and controls these tendencies. Furthermore, the development of moral censorship can be affected by the inability to overcome the Oedipus complex, which is much more difficult for the female sex, since men resolve it through their fear of castration, which does not exist in a woman.

On the other hand, suffering has become an inherent part of feminine nature and is even idealized and glorified as self-negation and sacrifice.

The following attitudes are readily observable and can easily be defined as being masochistic:

- Inhibitions expressed directly through demands and aggression
- Considering oneself weak, unworthy, or inferior, and at the same time implicitly demanding to be considered and to receive special treatment
- Emotional dependence on the opposite sex
- Exhibiting a tendency toward self-sacrifice, submission, a feeling of being used or of letting oneself be exploited, loading responsibilities onto men
- Using weakness and helplessness to conquer and dominate the opposite sex

There are also other physical factors that tend to favor masochistic mechanisms in women:

- Men are physically stronger. Less strength leads to masochistic roles.
- The possibility of rape as a direct consequence of the above point; this may bring about fantasies of being attacked, dominated, and injured.
- Menstruation, deflowering, and birth, are bloody processes that contribute to feelings of masochism.
- Female passivity during the sexual act. A woman is penetrated by the man. This could be interpreted as masochism.

Jealousy is an offshoot of masochism because it is a twisted way of stimulating the libido. By imagining erotic scenes of a husband and a rival, a woman stimulates her libido in a very painful way. Nevertheless, through this mechanism, pleasure and pain become entwined and the outcome is a perverted form of enjoyment—a mixture of pain and pleasure. When this mechanism is firmly installed in a woman's psyche, she will try to provoke opportunities to stimulate her jealousy in order to maintain the level of masochistic pleasure that she has become used to. At those moments language becomes very important because insults and blame are used for self-eroticization to intensify pleasure. Often, such scenes start off with hidden reproaches and mutate into violent recriminations, ending in hurtful insults. Throughout, a perverted orgasm can be reached. Afterwards, tears and depression usually follow due to the relaxation of tension.

Men feel completely disoriented after this psychic juggling has taken place. They probably do not even realize that what their partner is really seeking is to perpetuate her suffering and the feeling of being betrayed in order to hold onto feelings of masochistic satisfaction.

This is clearly a hellish trap; if the disagreements continue unabated, the marriage will be destroyed. On the other hand, if conditions are such that the woman cannot argue infidelity because the physical evidence tells a different story, she might become increasingly anxious and dissatisfied, and end by breaking all emotional links to her husband.

The masochistic impulse comes from a woman's feeling of dependence on men, from her feelings of inferiority with respect to men, and from her feelings of humiliation because, other than motherhood, she does not have access to society's most important roles. It is extremely important to understand how this masochistic impulse goes against a woman's attempts at emancipation. Indeed, if she were able to free herself, the satisfaction she derives from masochism would end. That is why it is important not to reject with thoughts and words that the heart desires.

## DIFFICULTY IN HAVING AN HONEST RELATIONSHIP WITH MEN

Honest communication can be defined as follows: it must exclude any intention to control or to use the other person for one's own purposes; one must put aside the desire to maintain a fake image of oneself; there needs to be real psychic opening in order to tell the truth; one must renounce possessive egotism that threatens to overpower one's partner as if he or she were an object.

Emotional openness is also indispensable to be able to communicate deeply otherwise the relationship will be superficial.

Unlike men, women adopt positions of exaggerated and tenacious defensiveness, employing the well-known art of concealment to avoid showing their real personalities. By means of a multitude of disguises, they pursue a single objective: to get to know the man without revealing who they really are.

What makes women use this tactic?

They want to hold on to a fictitious safety because, if they show themselves and open themselves fully, they can become vulnerable to criticism. Many women fear this. They could also be afraid of abandonment, betrayal, or rejection, all feelings that originate from inferiority, which comes from her sense of lacking. In fact it is logical that, when one feels weak one also feels a need to protect oneself artificially in order to counter-attack the feeling of vulnerability.

In his book, *The Language of Feelings*, David Viscott states the following: "Those who are incapable of accepting being hurt are also incapable of giving pleasure to others. Both processes demand openness. Being open means being vulnerable, capable of feeling hurt, but also of giving pleasure."

There is no contradiction between masochism and the fear of being hurt. When narcissism opposes masochism in the quest for balance, it is precisely the desire for balance at all costs that makes it difficult to be open and to wholeheartedly give of oneself.

Usually, men open their hearts to women, showing themselves without reservation. Women tend to tell light stories that contain only a touch of truth. That is how they satisfy their profound need to be idealized by men.

Relationships between women are also not honest because, as was outlined before, all women are rivals, each one fighting to possess a man. This attitude keeps the mechanisms of fear, envy and distrust alive. It is said that "no one knows a woman better than another woman." Behind this saying lies a latent fear of being unmasked. On the other hand, the female collective is a constant reminder of a woman's own perceived sexual inferiority. The abundance of castrated beings ensures a considerable level of anguish as women automatically compare and see the opposite taking place with men. Because of this, there exists a profound aversion deep inside. This also explains the difficulty that women's movements have in staying together because, even though they might unite to intensely defend their rights, they are easily divided to form rival subgroups.

In conclusion, women generally do not open up to men to honestly communicate with them because of their hidden aggression and envy. Women overflow emotionally only when they cannot handle it any more due to certain pressures from significant events. Women also do not wholeheartedly give themselves to others of the same gender because of the natural enmity that arises over the fight for men.

Above all, these attitudes prove the lack of confidence a woman has in herself. She projects her feelings and it makes her distrust everyone. The cover up, the defensive position, and the pretense are all weapons to protect her psychic fragility. It is easy to understand, therefore, why a woman would try to raise her self-esteem by valuing herself as an erotic object.

As you can see, the retreat of a woman's "I" hinders freedom in her relationships, and freedom is an indispensable element for truly seeing reality and developing individually.

# CONFUSION BETWEEN BEING
# FEMALE AND BEING FEMININE

Women have never really been women, only female. Their role is defined as that of a female, not as a human being of the female gender. Unfortunately, femininity is often confused with organic sexuality, and yet, these are completely different phenomena. Being female, with all that this entails biologically, is something that is acquired at birth. It is a gracious gift bestowed by nature effortlessly and without a woman's participation or choice.

The biological characteristics of female *Homo sapiens* are well-defined and well-known. On the other hand, the authentic condition of being feminine—the essence of what it really means to be a woman—is not known, understood or clearly defined. Unfortunately, femininity has been identified with a woman's ability to be erotically attractive. It is linked to the belief that by acting libidinously, a woman can prove her femininity. This originated the myth of the vamp. A vamp exhibits her female attributes with such generosity that the world comes to see her as the archetype of a super woman. She stands as a role model that the whole female gender tries to emulate in order to become more feminine. So many women believe that by using the same makeup, clothes, and hairstyles of movie stars, they will become more feminine, but they are only really dressing up as women without increasing their femininity in any way. On the other hand, as females, they will have increased their degree of erotic attractiveness and intensified their narcissistic satisfaction and the possibilities of catching a man (even if it does not mean that they will be able to hold onto him due to the ephemeral bond of sexual attraction).

The evolution of women, with reference to the female gender, is halted at the female animal level. What this means is that women only exist as female *Homo sapiens*. Their passive polarity or female identity is operative only biologically, like the female of any animal species. They have not become superior as feminine human beings. A woman's intelligence, feelings and capabilities, are equal to those of men, but they lack feminine definition. They are physically women but psychically undefined. This explains why women copy masculine roles because they are not familiar with the fundamental sexuality within their own psyches.

That is why women use their raw physical attractiveness, effectively adopting the look of attractive erotic bait. The result is an insane competition to undress, but using a great deal of artistry, so that it does not appear to be nudity. The pages of newspapers and magazines are jammed with an endless variety of images of erotic costumes. The females of the world seem to be trying to become women with such a pressing level of anxiety, yet unfortunately, they do no more than exalt and emphasize their libidinous sides.

Women lack a feminine "I." They only possess a female "I." The latter is only useful for motherhood as well as for sexual attraction and for inventing tricks to catch a man in order to satisfy one's own vanity.

The primitive erotic "I" is small and it only takes up a small part of the personality. Men also have an erotic "I," but it is located within their male "I." That gives them a psychic identity. Thus, a man's machismo forms only a part of his psyche. Women, on the other hand, have only one psychological area, reduced to the female "I," which represents their biological gender. The rest of their psychic structure is undefined. This is where they imitate and adopt masculine roles, thus alienating themselves from their true natures.

Men have a male "I" that somehow remains stable throughout. The "I" of a woman is much more dependent on that which is external. That is why a woman's "I" does not have permanence or consistency because it is continuously shifting according to social and material changes. Throughout history, women's roles have always varied, whereas men's roles have remained stable overall.

Unlike organic sexuality with which one is born, psychological femininity can only be obtained by enduring a slow and arduous process of individual development, not as a result of social conquests. Authentic femininity requires self-realization at the level of the "I," and thus it requires a person's own will to do so. It is a process of self-construction, not merely a process of receiving the values that emanate from social constructs. Such work must be done in the woman's inner world like an evolutionary change that stems from her own will. Furthermore, it has to do with an inner quality and not with external characteristics. Unfortunately, women who seek to be feminine through exalting their personal appearance and eroticism are wasting their time, and condemning themselves to failure as real women. In fact, such women will never exist as women, but only as females.

There are many other women who do not seek fulfillment through personal appearance and eroticism, but rather through careers or professional activities that require extensive use of their intelligence. Nevertheless, as was already mentioned, when they compete for important positions they are just copying male roles and, generally speaking, their motives are compulsive and not spontaneous. Their determination is not chosen freely; it is a neurotic anxiety to compensate for their lacks. It seems that women who are not considered to be physically beautiful according to society's rules will not be naturally inclined to act as erotic bait and will choose instead to excel intellectually or through other special abilities. Unfortunately, if they believe their unattractiveness, they might give up as women and try to fight men on their own turf by imitating male roles. If they feel externally unattractive, they might believe that they are unfeminine, and that they can only gain further advantages by surpassing men on their own territory. This battle can make them very masculine.

Some women who are both physically beautiful and very intelligent develop a masculine complex due to problems stemming from penis envy. These women are not content to be erotic bait; their personal expectations are driven by the anxious need to be important and to hold positions of power in order to compensate for their feelings of insecurity and inferiority with respect to men. A neurotic need to be independent can be as aberrant as the excessive dependence of a woman who attempts to live emotionally from a man.

Such independent women might achieve professional fulfillment, but not as an individual representative of the female gender. She might be physically a woman, but like a man mentally and psychologically in order to be able to compete successfully.

Unfortunately, we find that there are many women who manifest a clear relationship between independence and masculine behavior. It is somewhat shocking to see a beautiful woman who has a man's mental and emotional reactions. Often, such women are outstanding and successful, but the price they had to pay is to have become psychically masculine. They are psychologically male but sexually female.

I am convinced that the castration complex makes women develop strong aggression toward men. This emotional attitude raises their levels of testosterone above normal levels and makes them decidedly masculine. Without a doubt, there is a close relationship between testosterone levels and aggression. Testosterone makes a person aggressive. Conversely, if a woman's aggression is emotional, not hormonal, the production of testosterone is stimulated by this attitude.

Apparently, some women say that they prefer not to cultivate their intelligence but instead to act as erotic bait because of the cliché that men do not find intelligent women attractive. Maybe the reason is that men only know one type of intelligent woman, the masculine one, and this causes rejection towards them. It is rare to find a woman who balances intelligence with femininity. It is also said that men fear intelligent women because their mental development could signal the end of their male privileges. This argument does have some substance to it because machismo does exist, but an astute woman knows how to subtly prevent a man from feeling diminished.

Until a woman really develops her intellect, her field of interest will remain connected to beauty and physical attractiveness along with her maternal capacity, and these three aspects will define her role as a female.

"Woman" and "female" represent two different stages of development. The primitive female does not spontaneously become a woman. A female is a creation of nature. A woman must be the product of her own development. A woman is born from a female who decides to evolve and develop individually.

The crude reality that hinders equality between the sexes has thus been outlined: men have acquired psychic virility through the many pressing requirements of life, whereas their female counterparts have not developed their mental and psychic feminine identity, choosing instead to be defined only as females and as mothers. Due to this, males have a male role that remains in place over time and withstands historical changes. The current role of men is not very different from that of ancient times. On the other hand, women are geared more to the external; they are affected by a constantly changing outside world. Therefore, women anxiously pursue external things, changing and adapting to them. A good example of this is fashion, not only regarding clothes, hairstyles or makeup, but mostly with respect to other peoples' opinions. Women seem to have to adapt or follow what society or their partners expect from them, as well as adapt strategies in order to catch a man. If a woman marries a doctor, then she will be a bit of a doctor; the same thing with a politician; an intellectual will turn her into a thinker. A woman's identity as a person changes continually according to external requirements. As stated previously, this can be explained because women only have a sexual identity, whereas men have a sexual or generic "I," and another "I" that refers to them as individuals.

Whether a man is a tailor, a chef, or a dancer, he always maintains his sexual role even if his profession is traditionally one that women do. On the other hand, when women become politicians, soldiers, judges or have positions of authority or leadership, they usually copy male styles and it is difficult for them to act in a feminine manner.

Individually, every female must find her own identity as a woman-person, and this can only be achieved when she develops a stable and permanent center within her psyche. This center must remain constant within her intrinsic makeup, regardless of how her material world changes. Thus, through the creation of an adult and mature "I," she can totally fulfill herself as a woman and attain a perfectly defined feminine identity. This is achieved by focusing in on her internal world because that is how she can become aware of the forces that keep her alienated. When a woman is focused inwards, she can train herself to avoid being used by outside forces because she will have been strengthened by the conviction of how much damage those forces can wreak when she is invaded by them. Motivated by these observations, she can take hold of herself in order to resist those outside influences and become free. Whereas previously her psyche flowed due to temporary external stimuli, now she has the possibility to keep her psyche bound to the mandates from her own "I" in order to achieve psychological autonomy. *This coming of age is an essential requirement to achieving feminine realization.*

Here it is also important to define femininity and describe it in the most simple and objective manner possible, not as a model that must be adopted by force. Rather, one needs to understand femininity's intimate nature for one to know what needs to be developed in order to effectively be women. It is essential that women learn to truly value their own condition, and to understand that their supposed genital lack is nothing more than the outdated habit of using men as models. The reason for this is because, until now, the only feminine models that have been imitated are models of females. Models of women as individuals do not yet exist because they are still based on copying the masculine role.

It is a reality that women have penis envy. Why have women not learned to truly value their uteruses? Why do they unconsciously see it as a cavity, a void, or a lacking? Could it be because they sense that they only use their uterus in an erotic and maternal capacity? They have not been able to sublimate their libido to create a higher uterine condition within, which is femininity. Femininity is in fact the product of the proper sublimation of the uterine libido, similar to the passiveness or receptiveness of universal Eros.

Each human ability and capacity contains in it an array of possibilities for action, which can vary from a small, specific area to the vastness of the total human structure. Each human ability can become minimized or expand prodigiously, depending on the intelligent direction of the "I." This means that when the "I" has been formed in a conscious, superior, and mature manner, it can actively govern the abilities of the human body, taking them, if so desired, to a higher development or performance.

It is not necessary to prove or show the uterus's expansive capacities. Women only handle their sexuality as females and are absolutely unaware of the superior possibilities of what it means to be a uterine woman.

I think men have been able to sublimate their libido more than women. This is not a great achievement on their part, however, since it is due to a lucky combination of factors, not personal merit. This process will be better understood when we compare the basic erotic activity of males to that of females. Females, just like the egg, are fundamentally passive and receptive, whereas males, just like sperm are active, aggressive, and penetrating. Male eroticism is a force that is forever seeking, active, and fertile. Female eroticism is embracing and conceptive. Women inadvertently play the part of the vestal, stimulating both perceptively and visually a force that is expansive by nature. Erotically speaking, a woman is a uterus that takes in energy, compresses it and makes it dense, until it forms the matter of life. Women have the genetic memory to form living beings within themselves. The man is a phallus that irradiates and energizes, depositing the seed of life. The female gender internalizes; the male gender exteriorizes. The life force in the female gender tends toward the formation of matter; in the male gender, the drive is to impregnate with seed.

Women have fewer possibilities to sublimate their libidos because sublimation implies that erotic energy must flow through higher channels, not through purely biological ones.

Many great Renaissance painters were known to have sublimated their libido, concentrating their energy on their artistic creations rather than on genital activity. In this way, the force that did not flow through their biological channels flowed through mentally creative channels. It is even conceivable that some Renaissance painters were cognizant of the benefits of sublimation. In certain ancient knightly orders, a knight would deliberately choose a lady of great beauty and nobility and place his sword at her service, just like King Arthur and Sir Lancelot even though he failed. Lancelot declared love for the wife of his king for all eternity.

These declarations and types of relationships were very common in those times, and we can only understand them as a way to deliberately produce a higher flow of virile energy in order to sublimate the libido.

Men who have experienced platonic love have unwittingly practiced some kind of sublimation of their libidos. I am referring, of course, to men who are sufficiently clean to avoid the damage caused by lust.

Why can we not say the same for women? First of all, since it seems that women are a great deal more repressed than men, they are therefore unable to direct the energy that should be sublimated because it is stagnant in them. Secondly, as has been stated previously, sexual development in women is considerably more elaborate and complex than in men. The object of a man's love is always the woman (first the mother and then the wife), and men also only have one erogenous zone – the penis. Women, in contrast, need to change the object of their affection by transferring the love they feel for the mother to the father. Women also need to switch erogenous zones by moving the sensitivity of the clitoris to the vagina. This entire process consumes an enormous amount of psychic and libidinous energy, which in turn diminishes the flow of energy that can be sublimated.

Women have greater difficulty in overcoming the Oedipus complex because they do not fear castration, while the fear of castration in men is a principle motivator for them to overcome this complex. As a result, this complex is solved later for women, and often incompletely. The direct result of this slow process is that the creation of the Superior "I," a system of moral norms and values that drive a person toward perfection, is defective. Logically, the impulse toward sublimation is then also weak because the woman does not perceive the ideal goal to pursue. Obviously, without clear motivation on what is to be gained, it is not possible to progress. Since there is no easily identifiable goal and they are not driven by their Superior "I's," women tend to base all their progress on external and material achievements rather than on inner development.

On the other hand, when women are inextricably bound to their personal narcissism, they are extremely self-centered, which prevents them from opening up to the influence of male virile energy. When a woman falls in love with a man, it is seldom platonic, and she usually expects to convert this attraction into a permanent union. Her attraction is usually related to attaining personal security, the desire to have a child, or to catch a man, so as to overcome the anxiety caused by the lack of a penis.

Lastly, as women have been socialized to repress their sexuality and consider its free expression as something inappropriate or immoral, there have always been more men eager for sex and less women ready to satisfy them. Presumably that is why prostitution came into existence. Many men have been forced to invent a caricature of sublimation when faced with the difficulty of satisfying their erotic desires. It is necessary to point out, however, that here I am referring to a primitive and incomplete form of sublimation that is born from the admiration felt toward women. It is possible that in this process, men feel envy for the uterus, and that sublimation starts with the positive flow of envy, which is love.

Theodore Reik maintained that love always begins with envy or the negative flow of admiration. According to this criterion, men with baser instincts do not sublimate their libidos; they only covet a woman's body to satisfy carnal appetites. Admiration and love are not part of the equation.

With regard to sexual repression in women—as an obstacle to sublimation—it is necessary to point out that a petrified and stagnant libido represents a force that is halted, perturbed, handicapped, and diminished. This makes it difficult to direct energy toward higher levels, especially considering that there is not even enough energy at regular levels.

All sublimation must start with a stimulus to the libido, after which the energy that has been released rises, is repressed or descends, depending on the direction given to it by one's feelings and one's state of consciousness.

When repression exists, there is an increase in sterile libidinous pressure that ends up flowing unnaturally via mechanisms of hysteria or perverse pleasure, such as excessive talking, jealousy, imaginative eroticism, and the exaggerated intensification of dramatic feelings which are unconscious forms of psychic masturbation.

Feminine idealization of women as earthly and divine mothers, natural admiration for their beauty, awe at a woman's ability to create living beings, and the expectant erotic yearning generated by her female quality, has made men unconsciously see women as a kind of mother, goddess and lover, which, in many cases, has helped them sublimate their libidinous impulses toward a higher direction.

It is rare to find a man who does not admire women, as all men have had a mother.

On the other hand, the attitude of women toward men is not always one of positive admiration. More likely, it is one of envy, which can easily lead to an attitude of contempt for men's amorous needs. It is quite common to hear women say that "men are pigs"; "all they want is sex"; "men just take advantage of women," etc.

Another point to consider is that there are not many men worthy of a woman's admiration beyond their external values. Therefore, women do not usually admire men from deep inside of themselves, making sublimation more difficult.

The many problems and challenges of men's lives oblige them to develop a virile "I", which is stable, that is, a non-sexual male identity as a person of the male gender. Women lack this feminine "I" with regard to being a person; they only have a female "I."

With regard to the libido, the strong desire that males feel to possess a female can in some cases lead them to sublimate their desire—albeit in a completely unconscious manner—which strengthens their psychic male "I" even further. This is one of the reasons behind the evolutionary difference between the sexes on a sexual, psychic, and mental level. It has helped males to become men, but has not helped females to become feminine women. Men, to a certain extent, have mentalized their phallus, but women have not mentalized their uteruses, preferring to remain uterine females instead of accessing and consciously employing their higher sexuality.

# WHAT IS AUTHENTIC FEMININITY?

Authentic femininity is the evolution of a human female into a feminine person. False femininity is linked to what we know as female *Homo sapiens*, identified as such only because of her biological sexuality.

Without a doubt, superior femininity and self-fulfillment can only be the result of a combination of natural genetic factors and individual work. Naturally, this process involves willpower and is not spontaneous. This path is extremely steep, not flat.

In order to understand femininity, it is first necessary to analyze women in their most simple and primitive form: as a womb that conceives. When this quality is projected onto her personal identity, it can give us a key to understanding what it really means to be a woman. A woman's essential nature is receptive, embracing, retaining, and conceiving. At the level of female, this has to do with biological maternity. Raised to a higher level, it must engender authentic femininity.

In Nature nothing exists as a single unit; everything has its opposite and its complement. As we research femininity, it is useful to compare and contrast it with masculine virility, assuming these qualities are complementary opposites of each other. It might be easier to first briefly define virility, and then its opposite quality. For example, light can only be perceived because of darkness, heat because of cold, and relaxation because of tension. With respect to the last example, relaxation occurs when tension is eliminated.

I do not wish to utilize paternalistic criteria to analyze femininity through masculine references. On the contrary, it is about defining the psychic gender of the biological male and female in a balanced and harmonious way. Virility is a good place to start simply because it is a concept that is known and accepted worldwide—and even sometimes copied by women when they adopt masculine roles.

What is virility from a mental and psychological point of view? According to my research, I believe it manifests as willpower, as a powerful and sustained impulse to carry out what one wants. It is will, manifested through a Superior "I," which directs and controls an individual's faculties, such as sublimation of libidinous impulses toward overcoming the challenges of life. It is male aggression sublimated and directed with intelligence. This represents the generic male identity from a non-genital point of view.

The polar counterpart of non-genital virility that we have defined as will in men is called psychological femininity in women. It seems that women have not developed an equivalent capacity—what we call *will* in men—inasmuch as it corresponds to their inner world.

I have often pointed out that women live for and adore everything that is external; all their interests are based on cultivating physical appearance, and evaluating everything according to it, not because of essential content. Women continuously and irreparably turn the "I" to face outward, separating from her *self* to identify with male roles and subjecting her internal state to external circumstances. Culture becomes superficial like this, and socially transcendental things are ignored during the anxious pursuit of catching a man. In other words, a woman does not live by herself and for herself; she lives in function of a man.

Women, lacking an inner world, unsuccessfully chase happiness though the fleeting stimulus of pleasure. This is so poor and ephemeral a reward that it needs to be continuously renewed in order to sustain a sufficient level of sensorial satisfaction. In the end the worst kind of boredom is created.

When a woman has not yet developed her inner world, she lives through the amorous adventures of other women, projecting their stories onto her own life and living vicariously through their experiences and the details of their lives. Her female role models are movie stars, models, and famous artists.

When a woman has not developed her inner world, her "I" does not exist as a person but merely as an erotic object. Unfortunately, most women remain like this, cultivating only their physical appearance, dressing as women, but copying the pseudo, sexy, femme fatale role models that abound. Such women, whether deliberately or not, concentrate all their expectations in life on looking like good erotic bait in order to catch a man and in order to sufficiently satisfy their narcissism. This silly game often consumes the greater part of a woman's life and she might not realize that because of it she will not have enough time or strength to fulfill herself and will be obliged to settle for remaining a female or a mere imitation of a man.

With regard to her sexuality, a female *Homo sapiens* only recognizes the reproductive capacity of her vagina and uterus, not her psychological capacity, which has to do with the flow of libidinous energy on a higher level. The capacity to conceive children is the external physical manifestation of female sexuality; the creation, development, and control over one's inner world is the higher realization of genuine femininity. The vagina and the uterus must not only exist physically, but must also become real in a woman's psyche as a resource that forms her inner world. This is genital femininity projected into the psyche.

A female *Homo sapiens* who does not emphasize her erotic attraction can create herself as a woman from her psychic uterus through which she can consciously elaborate her experiences *within* to form and develop an independent "I." This can only be achieved if she is convinced that it is necessary to become a woman, if she understands the correct methodology for introspection, if she lives through her many experiences and takes total responsibility for them, and if she faces the results of her actions in an absolutely independent way. By doing so, she can capitalize on meaningful experiences that are in reality food for the "I."

The Superior "I" must be formed consciously. This is quite different from the way the common psychological "I" is formed. The latter is developed gradually as a part of the psyche, influenced and shaped by society. Even though the psychological "I" is one's personal identity, underneath it all, it is nothing more than a projection of humanity's social identity. All men and women are children of mother society, but if one wishes to obtain authentic individuality and real psychological autonomy, one must create something that is one's own, something that is formed by one's consciousness and distilled by one's higher rationality. Otherwise, one will not be any different from the herd. More than anything else, *women need to become mothers to themselves*, focusing their maternal capacities on their own person, taking themselves under their own wings, teaching and transforming themselves through the art of femininity.

When a woman's "I" is developed and mature, she should be able to radically change mechanisms that traditionally hinder her evolution. Narcissism, for example, originated as compensation for a feeling of inferiority with respect to men. The mechanism of narcissism needs to work continuously to keep a woman's self-esteem high and generate sufficient self-confidence. For this mechanism to work, it must feed off external resources, such as the admiration she might inspire as erotic bait. When a woman realizes that her erotic attractiveness is declining, coupled with a loss of confidence and low feelings of self-worth, profound anxiety sets in.

The mechanism of self-esteem can be compared to a chimney that needs a continuous supply of wood (external energy) to keep combustion alive. Accordingly, the mechanism of self-esteem needs powerful external reinforcement to keep it functioning at a high level. Such external reinforcement needs to come from people who admire, support, nurture or caress the individual, since without this help the individual's narcissism feels threatened and a kind of depression sets in.

It is important to differentiate between *self-esteem* and *self-worth*. While self-esteem is a compulsive attempt to artificially strengthen an "I" that is weak, childish or dilapidated, self-worth represents the objective recognition of one's own value which is born from authentic development of an "I" that is self-sufficient and does not need external props. Self-esteem artificially creates an inflated "I" that is quite puny with regard to its real potential. Real self-esteem is achieved when a strong, powerful, valuable and non-selfish "I" is developed, since it does not need to feed off flattery or vanity because it knows its own worth perfectly well.

The selfish "I" is a compulsive identity, formed from a neurotic defensive need. In other words, it is formed from the wish to compensate for one's own lacking by resorting to symbols of power that artificially magnify one's own smallness. The "I" that is born from conscious introspection does not have a compulsive mechanism. It acts naturally and spontaneously. It has become an autonomous resource of the will.

Paternalism and cultural influences affect how strongly emotionally dependent little girls are. Because of these influences, little girls remain emotionally dependent for a lot longer and more fervently than little boys. That is why for most of their lives little girls value their "I" according to the guidelines of others. They desperately need the approval of others, fearing that without it, they might be rejected or deprived of love and tenderness. When women truly develop an "I" and an inner world, they are no longer dependent on the opinions of others and are more confident in their own ability to judge. This is the moment that a woman can consider herself emancipated and independent from men. It does not mean she will reject or compete with men's abilities or values. On the contrary, once a woman is free and possesses her own feminine identity, she is able to relate to men in a non-compulsive way, seeking a man's company as a complement in love, and not making him responsible for her happiness and fulfillment. Nor will she approach him with the idea of symbolically appropriating his coveted penis. As a fully responsible adult, she has earned her right to equality with the opposite sex. This achievement cannot be relinquished, nor can it be taken away by any human or divine power.

If she is able to achieve this, she will have no need to copy male roles since she will be an abundantly feminine woman who accepts and enjoys her feminine condition, and perceives herself as an autonomous, highly evolved, and psychologically independent being. Because she will be free from the psychic slavery of phallic symbolism, she will be able to exercise her freedom as an equal to men.

Imagine the tremendous amount of psychic energy that will be released and recuperated when women resolve their basic conflict of feeling devalued with respect to men. They will no longer need to act out the narcissistic mechanism of self-gratification because it will have been replaced by a healthy and natural satisfaction derived from the perception of themselves as truly valuable and developed beings. Once a woman's anguished need to appear important, loved, and appreciated for neurotic reasons disappears, as well as the compulsive and exhausting need to adorn herself as erotic bait, all the stagnant energy that was stuck because of her internal contradictions can be recovered. This new force can now be used freely to obtain non-neurotic objectives. Needless to say, it will then be much easier for a woman to achieve her goals since she will no longer be held back by her own struggle. Obviously, the greater the energy one is able to focus on what one wants the greater the possibilities of obtaining it.

However, it is not enough to create a favorable internal world for femininity to bloom magically; it is also important to know what to do with this internal world. It is not a gold thread of femininity, but more like a center for creation, control, and development of an adult and feminine woman. Therefore, it is necessary to define behaviors that can be considered feminine, and to determine what femininity really is without trying to forcefully impose a model onto anyone. Comprehension is important because when a person really understands what is wrong with one's current behavior and is able to clearly visualize the tremendous advantages gained from behaving correctly, it is not very difficult to change one's conduct. In fact, it will happen almost naturally, almost as if metaphorically one was walking down the street consciously avoiding the potholes or seeking refuge when it rains. It is important to remember that each wrong behavior hides some lack of comprehension about one's vital experiences in life. The feminine model herein defined is not to be imitated or adopted by force, whether dogmatically through imitation or without reflection. This model does not intend to distort or eradicate a woman's regular everyday behavior, but rather, it is about developing the awareness of what it means to be a woman. Once the essence of this phenomenon is understood, femininity can be achieved and comprehended individually, not because of a stereotype or because of imitation.

What does it mean to be feminine? What does a woman need to become feminine?

There are three possible manifestations of femininity:

1.  Natural or genetic femininity bestowed by nature
2.  Cultural or socialized femininity can be defined as genetically manipulated and contaminated femininity concerning its natural purity
3.  Superior femininity: consciously and deliberately conceived in the woman's psychic uterus

The first kind of femininity represents the natural outcome of being a female *Homo sapiens* without culture. It is an active, conceiving instinct, a womb that catches the seed to make it grow. It is fertile land incarnate, manifesting all of its transformative and creative powers. It is the conceiving instinct of Mother Nature. It therefore lacks discrimination and conceives everything that has penetrated the egg without differentiation. This is how it has been for all women across history, time, races, and cultures.

The second kind of femininity corresponds to a forced internalization of cultural and behavioral rules that society has outlined for women, which vary according to era and geographic location. Under social influences, the purely instinctive female loses a large part of her essential wisdom. This process is similar to a lion cub that is tamed in order to live with humans, altering its sense of smell, orientation, and hunter instinct.

Accordingly, nature's wisdom becomes buried under and contaminated by prejudices and taboos and by the compelling need to adapt to neurotic social systems. When we refer to the female *Homo sapiens* as the most primitive manifestation of a possible transition within the evolutionary process, we are talking about the socialized female, not about femininity in its pure state.

The third kind of femininity—superior femininity—is the possible result of conscious management of both the cultural and natural aspects of femininity. By conducting research and analysis, women can take what is appropriate and convenient from both aspects of femininity, and reject what is extraneous.

There are several considerations that must be met to be considered a truly feminine woman:

- *Understand what motivates one to act as a female rather than as a woman.* Clearly define within one's own thoughts what it is to be a female and what it is to be a woman. There is no other way for a woman to truly see herself and to have the necessary motivation to change.

- *Understand that the transition toward femininity is not an easy process.* One will need to become intellectually active to be able to control oneself, and to be able to discern the obstacles that prevent one from being authentically feminine.

- *Accept being a woman,* not in the sense of resigning oneself to being a woman, but rather in the sense of feeling truly satisfied with this condition and really appreciating what it means to be able to conceive on a physical and psychic level. This means that one needs to relinquish penis envy and eliminate the myth of the phallus, reject its neurotic value, and become aware of having something of similar value—the psychic uterus—but with complementary capacities.

- *Abstain from imitating masculine roles and avoid neurotic competition with men.* This refers to the compulsive need to prove that one can be as intelligent, important, efficient, and well prepared as men. However, it is not wrong to compete in a healthy way without envy or resentment and without unconscious impulses to humiliate or degrade men, just the personal desire to reach a higher individual level through the best use of one's abilities.

- *Accept passivity in the real sense of the word as the main feminine condition.* José A. Infante in an article entitled *Feminine Sexuality,* published in a Chilean Magazine of Psychoanalysis in 1980, said the following: "We refer to the concept of passiveness pointed out by Freud as one of the predominant characteristics of femininity, and compared it with what we believe to be a more adequate expression: *receptiveness.* Passiveness is defined as receiving an action from an agent without cooperating with that agent, in other words, letting others do without doing anything for oneself. Receptiveness, however, is all of the following: the ability to take what one is given or sent; to perceive; to sustain; to hold a body to another; to suffer the damage another person does to you or damage that just happens to you by chance; to admit something within oneself; to admit, approve, and accept something; to accept someone into one's company or community; to wait or to face any attack with intention to resist and reject it."

Described in this way, passiveness implies being an object, while receptiveness can only imply being a subject.

Nevertheless, to be receptive and welcoming is also a quality of the human female, so it becomes necessary to understand the difference between how the female views receptiveness opposed to how a woman does.

The key to this difference lies in the conscious discrimination that a woman must make to freely determine what she will receive, how much of it, and for what purpose.

- *Attain one's own identity that is the result of the woman's individual development.* Each woman must be an individual before all else. Therefore, she must give up belonging to a sort of female trade union that exists in everyday reality, that is, the tendency of women to come together spontaneously and form a common front against men, defending each other and sharing numerous prejudices as if they were secrets.

These cliques get together to discuss all kinds of weird recipes or methods for catching or holding onto a man, or for not letting oneself be overwhelmed by men. Unfortunately, this inadvertently creates a sort of psychological mob and brings out the worst qualities of the species, rendering the good intentions of the group's members unproductive. Moreover, individual responsibility, which is important if one is to develop one's "I," is diluted in a group. This does not mean that one must not have a social life, but one must not let oneself be negatively influenced by other people's prejudices. To develop a strong "I," one must learn to autonomously make decisions for oneself according to one's good judgment.

- *Develop a rational thought pattern through all possible avenues, thus sharpening one's intelligence.* Until women are able to abandon their frivolous attitudes and superficial analyses that they are known for, they will not be able to take care of themselves. In order to face life's challenges independently, a woman will need to muster all her intelligence. Knowing that someone else would come to her rescue when faced with difficulties has hindered the development of a woman's capabilities. To become responsible for oneself and one's own destiny is the best way to become a woman. This must, however, be accomplished without compulsion or prejudice. A woman must use her everyday experiences constructively, otherwise she may get prematurely frustrated at the first sign of difficulty of a certain importance.

- *Purify or cleanse one's genetic or natural femininity.* As was already mentioned, genetic femininity is contaminated by cultural influences which unfortunately contain the elements that provoke passions and human perversion. Thus, envy, hatred, pride, destruction, jealousy, and selfishness are almost inextricably mixed up in the hearts of men and women, giving rise to all kinds of misfortunes in an individual's destiny and interpersonal relationships.

In relation to this, ancient philosophers declared that "one must clean one's own 'container' before one is able to love." This applies particularly to women because they have been socialized to express their feelings much more freely than men, which makes it much easier for them to hurt themselves or to hurt others. On the other hand, in the same way that the world of rational thought is the center of masculine activity, feelings, emotional intuition, and psychic sensibility are the instruments by which the feminine psyche manifests itself. In this way a woman is more natural than a man, and can therefore be a lot more impulsive, vehement, and excitable, thus amplifying passions that also affect men.

Emotional sensibility is the link that unites a woman to nature, but as it is nonspecific or neutral in its essence, it may manifest constructively or destructively. It may give life, love, harmony, and peace, or irradiate hatred and destruction. It is obvious that this range not only affects the environment that surrounds a woman, but also her own existence in a very decisive way.

In fact, a woman's emotional sensibility is where she has direct contact with natural or genetic femininity. This is where the memory of nature lies. So, depending on her emotional states, she herself directs the force of her libido either constructively or destructively. Therefore, it is of utmost importance to clean her container, to purify feelings, to get rid of resentment, hatred, envy, aggression, and all expressions of destruction.

Psychologists maintain that it is natural that a person hate, be envious, feel resentment and aggression, since one should not artificially repress such manifestations. I maintain, however, that this is only valid for people who have not sublimated their libido (the majority of people), who have kept their emotional sensibility in a primitive state.

Sublimation does not annul aggression, hatred or violence. Sublimation channels these energies through a superior level of expression and converts them into a docile force for the "I" to handle. The completely sovereign and conscious "I" can then decide what to do with them. Whereas before the individual was constantly swept by, possessed, and obliged to adhere to the dominant instinctive power, now the same individual can take possession of this force, handle it and control it at will.

Only two types of manifestations of feelings exist: positive or negative, constructive or destructive. The positive is the expression of Eros; the negative is the expression of Thanatos.

The individual, through personal inner choice, can choose one expression or the other. It is like when a person wants to go to the movies and can choose to watch a horror movie, a drama, a story of passion, or a happy, light, and enjoyable movie that will make one feel better. The individual must decide what he or she wishes to do with his or her emotions: build or destroy.

I am convinced that, regardless of the experiences a person has had, a person can choose to be aggressive, hateful, destructive, and resentful, or welcoming, fraternal, tolerant, and open to others. It is the internal attitude of the individual and one's negative or positive disposition regarding every day events that makes the difference.

One can control one's inner disposition through higher rationality, as opposed to unchecked emotions, in order to positively orient oneself. One's inner desire can be controlled by one instead of letting oneself be manipulated by it. One only needs to understand that destruction and hatred only engender death and devastation, and yield very negative dividends to want to change this passionate state.

When one clearly understands which personal behavior is harmful to one's own interests, and what one cannot obtain as a result, one can change and modify one's behavior by directing one's interest towards positive goals that can be achieved.

The seed of one's own destruction lies within hatred, envy, negativity and destructive emotions because these kinds of emotions are not productive and only cause destruction.

Personal control can be achieved by managing inner emotional attitudes. This does not mean through repression, which is a process imposed from the outside onto the inner world of an individual. Sublimation, on the other hand, commences from one's inner world, and is born from understanding, a sense or vision of something, or conviction. This gives rise to an expansive force that begins to flow to the inside. In this way, change originates in one's inner world, not because it is imposed from the outside.

- *Project outwards*. Women live continuously projected toward the outside, waiting for what they want to come to them from the outside world.

This attitude is one of constant expectation: hoping to find a man; hoping for good luck; hoping for a miracle from the Holy Mother or some saint; expecting society to protect her with special laws; hoping her children will make her happy and satisfy her inner needs; expecting to be loved, idealized, and supported; and, constantly expecting changes to take place in her life due to good luck, the influence of the stars, or some favorable event. That is why women feel so strongly identified with love stories, dreaming that they are the main characters. When a woman visits a fortuneteller, it is as if she wants to be shown her destiny and is inadvertently admitting her impotence to create something by herself.

It would seem as if women have no future and are looking for existential things to fill the future. This also makes them dream because they playfully fantasize about situations they would like to experience. Instead of building a real, positive destiny, women let their fantasy fly to imagine certain things coming into their lives. Within her behavior resides the concept of *attracting* instead of the concept of *doing*. That is why they spend so much time and energy taking care of their physical appearance in order to be good erotic bait, expecting (and always waiting) to catch a man with the expectation that he will make them happy. When they find the individual they looking for, they transfer the responsibility for their own happiness to him, blaming him for not fulfilling—since it hardly ever happens—their expected level of satisfaction.

It is clear to see that the activities described above are useless for women. Everything they do daily, such as making themselves beautiful, improving their figures, being fashionably dressed, only represent a kind of a hook, the hope of catching (that is, attracting from the outside), company, love, happiness, satisfaction, security, and pleasure. While a woman completely devotes herself to such activity, she is in fact totally disregarding her development as a human person, choosing to be an erotic object, not a human subject. By trying to possess a man, pleasure, security, and happiness, women inevitably lose themselves, since they do not achieve a real existence as individuals.

Projecting outwards makes a woman dependent, vulnerable, and needy for external events to be favorable, without realizing that she can create her own destiny, as men do. Otherwise, she is not forming or developing herself, especially if she expects to solve her problems by attracting people who will solve them for her. She does not understand that she has the tools to overcome any inconvenience or difficulty, as well as to be happy through her own efforts, not as a result of favorable external events.

Time and time again, history has proven that the individual who cannot be happy by himself or herself will never be able to find happiness, even when external circumstances are favorable. It is essential to stop believing in the type of happiness that the fetus experiences in the womb where the creature has every physical and psychological need fulfilled immediately and continuously. Happiness—and I will never tire of repeating this—can only be real and everlasting when it originates from one's internal world and not as a result of favorable external circumstances. Generally, people expect external events to favor or determine their inner happiness. In reality, the contrary is much more probable, meaning that inner happiness and optimism will positively affect the material events of one's life.

Because of an unconscious conviction of their own weakness, women have a pathological fear of being abandoned by men who they view as providers of what they wish to acquire—through donation and not through personal effort, through living projected toward their partner instead of living in their individual inner worlds. Women who live like this cease to have an individual existence of their own and live emotionally though their partners, depriving their own "I," and dangerously invading the inner world of the men they are with, who in turn, feel stripped of their inner space and may end the relationship, motivated simply by a self-preservation instinct.

There are many women who will repeatedly fail in love because they try to fill themselves with the life they take from a man who often starts to feel a decrease in his vitality and consequently feels threatened.

Remember the difference between mature (true) and immature (false) love that Erich Fromm spoke about: "I love you because I need you" (immature love) and "I need you because I love you" (mature love).

The fundamental feature of authentic love is that it is not manipulative, nor does it depend solely on the need to satisfy one's own needs. It does not use the other person as a means to carry out personal ambitions, but allows the other to develop individually. That is why we can state that women—and men too—do not know how to love because the main motivation for having a relationship is to use their partner as a means to accomplish their own expectations. This is contrary to the genuine nature of love which is to give and be generous.

- *Resolving the Oedipus complex:* According to Freud, women suffer almost indefinitely under the weight of the Oedipus complex, and only abandon it very late in life, and even then, not completely. The presence of this complex noticeably stunts the formation of a superego.

Judith M. Bardwick, a fellow of the American Psychological Association, has written that: "A person with a mature superego has within a set of personal standards, and understands and values himself/herself independently from the value others give him/her. A person with a weak superego continues to value himself/herself as a child does, based on the reactions of other people, and behaves the way he/she foresees others will behave."

Freud stated that the superego of a woman is never as impersonal or independent as a man's is, and it is much less evolved because it depends on external sources. In other words, a woman's superego is dependent on the parents who punish or reward, or on other important people. Bardwick states that women clearly depend on third parties in order to create their self-esteem.

When the development of a woman's superego is disturbed by complexes, her development as an individual and independent person is notably hindered, leaving her very vulnerable to other people's opinions; her self-worth remains at childish levels and she will be extremely sensitive to affection and hostility. This prevents her from having her own opinion and from being able to decide for herself. It also fosters dependence, damages her sense of justice, and leaves her indifferent to cultural values.

It is easy to see that self-realization requires internal free will. It also requires rational thinking that is both conscious and autonomous. Such faculties must be managed and fostered through use of the will in a sustained and firm manner. This would mean putting an end to a passive *laissez faire* attitude, as well as the passive form of waiting for something before making a decision to act.

As has already been pointed out, the Oedipus complex consumes a great amount of psychic energy that one absolutely must recover if it is to be used creatively, instead of being wasted because of artificially having to maintain psychological homeostasis (that is, the state of remaining the same without generating new resources).

How does one resolve the Oedipus complex?

Elements of traditional psychoanalysis can be helpful, such as understanding the concept that a woman can replace the desire to have a penis with the desire to have a child. The attraction toward the father is based on the subconscious desire that he will give her the phallus denied to her by her mother. Since this desire then turns into a yearning to have a child with him, it is feasible to substitute this yearning with the impulse or conscious gestation or creation of a child. I recommend in this situation that a woman ardently seek a psychic gestation, not a biological one. It is advisable for each woman to decide to create herself as a new being in her psychic uterus, so that after some time has passed, she will be able to give birth to her own person, to a strong, independent, mature, and adult individual.

Motherhood offers more than just one option, and in fact, having a child of flesh and blood is just one. The force of motherhood can be used to create a being of flesh and blood or a being made from psychic energy, as referred to previously. A woman can overcome the Oedipus complex through individual development.

Logically, the longed for and long sought emancipation and recognition as an adult can only come about through the sculpting of oneself, not as the result of a spontaneous event at some point in time, nor as a result of legal recognition or external support that basically just legitimizes a woman's helplessness.

It is important to reflect that whatever role women perform in society, they will only be able to do so either as a product of their perfection, or as a product of their immaturity, and, if women persist in their attitude of not evolving individually, they will be denying their higher contribution to both themselves and to the world, thus avoiding their responsibilities.

A woman must also understand that as she forms and enhances her individual values, the feeling of lacking a penis will weaken and vanish, together with envy and resentment.

- *Changing the erogenous zone from the clitoris to the vagina:* I must admit that I hesitated before including this controversial subject on the list, considering that it is a traditional Freudian concept that was probably not well clarified by Freud himself. Masters and Johnson do not agree with this concept. They said that there cannot be a vaginal orgasm without a clitoral orgasm since they both make up a single anatomical entity. Their investigation indicated that the erotic potential of the clitoris is greater than that of the lower third part of the vagina, and that abandoning the stimulation of the clitoris in pursuit of a mature psychosexuality is unrealistic.

However, the physical response of the clitoris has not been evaluated properly to see if its response is a healthy response or a pathological one that has come to be considered normal. In fact, if statistical norms are used to determine criteria for health or sickness, various disturbances that affect the masses will not be taken into account.

Is vaginal insensitivity the result of a lack of nerve receptors present in this area? Or does vaginal insensitivity correspond to the somatizing of a psychological disturbance or immaturity?

In her work, *The Descent of Women*, Elaine Morgan made some interesting points with regard to this problem. She discussed the possibility that such phenomena may have happened as a result of the transition of the female from quadruped to biped. It made males change the position for copulation, thus changing the area of the vagina that was stimulated during intercourse. According to Masters and Johnson, the inner walls of the vagina do not have nerve endings and are insensitive. They proved this in experiments in which the inner walls of the vagina were softly caressed. Morgan states that if we consider that the main mechanism that triggers sexual activity in female cats, rhesus monkeys and most other higher quadrupeds is in the muscular tissue toward the lower or inner surface of the horizontal vagina, then what is needed for an orgasm would be energetic friction in the lower or ventral wall. This does not happen with the female *Homo sapiens* when she has intercourse facing her partner, unlike animals.

If we were to compare sexual excitement to an itch, it is easy to see how it cannot be relieved through soft stimulus, but rather through a fast and vigorous massage.

Dr. Arnold Kegel proved that sexual satisfaction increased spontaneously in women who practiced exercises that reinforced the coccyx pubic muscles that surround the vagina. In his studies, Kegel noted that some of the women who practiced his exercises increased their capacity for experiencing orgasms and sexual satisfaction for the first time in their marriages.

This approach is interesting, but my personal opinion is in line with what Freud asserted: psychosexual maturity depends on transferring clitoral sensitivity to the vagina. I believe, however, that he meant this in a more psychic context than physiologically because each organ of our body also forms part of our psychic structure, that is, every physiological function corresponds to a psychic one. This helps to understand psychosomatic disturbances better because of the connection between psychic and biological functions. When a psychic function is disturbed, biological disorder occurs.

Could it be that when a woman refuses to accept her femininity because of penis envy, she annuls the sensitivity of her vagina?

The clitoris appears as a rudimentary penis, left over from a remote time when sapiens were hermaphrodites. Anthropologists may be surprised to find out that man has existed on earth for much longer than is thought.

Putting these ideas aside, it is worth asking: What male organ complements the clitoris? Could it be the penis? Since men have no other sex organ other than the penis, can it be assumed that the most logical complement of the penis is the vagina?

I am of the belief that the clitoris is the seat of self-eroticism for immature women who have not learned to give themselves whole-heartedly, and that clitoral orgasm reflects a lack of feminine receptiveness. By that, I am referring to the orgasm restricted to the clitoris. This tiny appendage seems to be the manifestation of masculinity in women, an externally projecting force that expresses the yearning to impose rather than to receive. The vagina and the uterus, on the other hand, represent the capacity to receive and conceive. These qualities are truly feminine qualities.

If we continue our analysis from this point of view, it can be inferred that psychosexual maturity does not depend on making the vagina sensitive in order to experience vaginal orgasm as much as on becoming emotionally receptive and welcoming, psychologically accepting penetration like the function of a planter that must deposit a seed at a certain depth so that it will be able to grow. In this case the concern is not with the desire to procreate, but with the mechanism of intercourse.

It is not necessary to be focused on annulling clitoral sensitivity since, most likely, the erotic effects of the clitoris and the vagina will become spontaneously regulated when emotional resistance to penetration disappears. How much an orgasm is due to the vagina or the clitoris does not matter. What is important is that the woman accepts and values her receptive conceiving condition. It is highly probable that in this psychic state, vaginal sensitivity will increase considerably, which seemed impossible in the laboratory of Masters and Johnson.

It is important not to overlook the fact that male sexuality is medullar in nature, whereas the female sexual response depends greatly on the limbic system. Therefore, the influence of the emotions regarding the expectation and acceptance of being penetrated should not be ignored.

- *Creating a psychic uterus:* The psychic uterus offers the possibility to consciously use the psychic component of the uterus. This refers to its capacity to receive, to internalize, to develop, to transform, and to materialize, in other words…to give life. In the same way that a woman gives life to a child, she can use her conceiving power to self-create, self-develop and give birth to herself in order to stop being an object and to be able to truly exist as an individual.

It behooves me to insist that feminine emancipation is possible only at an individual level, which is to say, it can only be realized by firmly deciding to do so. That is why it is not necessary to ask men or the government for permission. It has to do with perfecting oneself and, since it directly favors human society and its higher values, no one should really oppose it.

Independence must be achieved without copying male roles. The search for a real feminine identity should gradually come about as the woman is de-alienated. In fact, feminine nature is alienated by and for men, so by becoming independent, a woman's femininity is released and flows freely.

The more a woman develops an independent, strong, and mature "I" and takes on the responsibilities for her own existence, learning to think for herself and ceasing to depend on other people's opinions, the more she will be able to find her own feminine condition.

The psychic uterus must be a kind of secret chamber where she can retreat regularly for periods of introspection in order to obtain self-knowledge, elevate her actions, and find the significance of her everyday experiences.

As the "I" is a mandatory point of reference in the psychic life of an individual, the aim of her introspection must be to nurture the "I" with the lessons taken from everyday life. Normally, people do not reflect on their experiences with enough care to be able to discover the true meaning of them. That is why they waste their lives since they are depriving themselves of evolving and of reaching maturity.

Normally, experiences are only lived at an emotional level, and the reasons behind one's problems or limitations are never understood. Inevitably, this translates into a lack of growth and development because a person can only become an adult when one takes charge of one's own life, preparing to successfully face the inevitable problems of everyday existence.

The purpose behind creating a psychic uterus is to reverse the woman's psychological consciousness so that her "I" stops being projected toward the outside and learns to dwell quite naturally within her. In this way, her "I" will get stronger because she will constantly be using her own criteria, judgment, and preference.

It is important to use one's "I" in order to convert it into an inner center that remains fixed and strong, so that when one says "I," one will always be referring to the same entity, not to a ubiquitous and variable being incapable of controlling a person's psychic system.

This "I" is superiorly formed, able to constantly maintain its intrinsic condition despite external fluctuations. The "I" must not change with events or the passing of time; it must only change if it is evolving.

This is how women will be able to anchor themselves internally and learn to value themselves and react independently.

This strong "I" will also allow a woman to solve her own problems, feel happy because she has decided to do so, and reach the goals she has set for herself in life. However, it is not possible for a woman to create an "I" with these characteristics if she does not enter into her inner world on a daily basis in order connect to herself constantly.

There are two possibilities in life: either life forms the individual with no possibility for the person to oppose its influence, or a person is able to adequately use the events of one's life to create a dynamic that is in harmony with one's most intimate desires. This is more empowering than the habitual way of thinking that positive events happen due to the grace of God or as a gift from nature, and that when everyday existence is unfavorable, the only thing to do is to resign oneself.

The woman must become conscious of the power that emanates from the psychic function of her uterus—the ability to project inside, to transform, to develop, and to materialize. This means that a woman must introject within her all the events that take place in her life, whatever they may be. She must work with them consciously in the alchemical laboratory of her inner world, and then give birth to them in a new, superior form. This capacity is exclusive to the feminine nature, and is the opposite and, at the same time, is the equivalent of a penis. Therefore it is a fundamental tool to becoming equal to men, not by taking away a man's value, but by equitably appreciating herself.

It is important to clarify that the psychic uterus is not a duplicate of the physical organ, nor can it be found anywhere in a woman. It simply corresponds to the psychic function of the uterus and is part of the whole psyche overall. Because of its receptive characteristics it can be used as the center of a woman's inner world. A woman can use her psychic uterus by practicing introspection.

It is essential to understand that within this creative inner space, passiveness is no longer inert; it takes on a life of its own and transforms the psychic center into the capacity to give.

Women will often have difficulty giving, and giving of themselves wholeheartedly, because giving is perceived as a loss and not as part of being fulfilled. The opposite is actually true. By frequently practicing conscious introspection, a woman can start to fill her inner world with new and rich elements and become more secure and strong. Gradually, she will be able to give, and give of herself wholeheartedly because she will no longer feel the anguished need to support her "I" with external props. She will cease feeling diminished because she will know her individual value perfectly well.

# THE OPTION OF MOTHERHOOD

Motherhood is one of the only female roles that has been universally accepted throughout the course of history. Women have been told that if they give birth, they will earn the same social respect that men receive for their cultural creations. Motherhood has been glorified with a mystic and divine halo over the course of the socialization process. The process of motherhood is seen as a renunciation of the woman's personal interest, a totally unselfish act, and the giving of life in a most sublime and detached manner.

Motherly love is generally equated with a sublime impulse that is within a woman's instincts that motivates her to make all types of sacrifices in order to achieve the individual realization of her children.

In order to attain the goals outlined thus far, to end discrimination against women and promote a woman's individual development, it is essential to demystify the role of motherhood in the way it is currently seen, since it is one of the main obstacles hindering a higher destiny for mankind.

A good place to begin is with several extracts from Elizabeth Badinter's work, *The Myth of Motherhood.*

"1780: Lenoir Police Deputy comments, not without bitterness, that of the twenty-one thousand children that are born every year in Paris, only one thousand are brought up by their mothers. Another privileged thousand are cared for by wet-nurses in their father's home. The rest go from their mother's breast to the more or less detached home of a paid wet-nurse... How can we explain the abandonment of a baby at a time when the mother's milk and care mean a greater possibility of survival? How can we explain such a lack of interest in the child that is the opposite of today's values...? Why did the indifference of the 18th Century become the over-protectiveness of the 19th and 20th Centuries? This change of maternal attitude contradicts the idea of a female and woman's instinct; it is a curious phenomenon... Maternal instinct is no longer an accepted concept. Motherly love is only a human feeling... When we remember the history of maternal attitudes, we become convinced that maternal instinct is a myth. We have not found any universal or necessary pattern of behavior in motherhood. On the contrary, we have proof of a great variability in a mother's feelings, depending on her culture, ambitions and frustrations. From all of this, we can only conclude that maternal love is only a feeling and as such essentially subjective, even though this conclusion seems cruel. This feeling may or may not exist; it can be given or it can disappear. It evidences strength or frailty. It may privilege one offspring or all the children. It all depends on the mother, her personal history, and history itself."

Badinter's research shows us how a mother's attitude toward her child has changed dramatically throughout history, and how the current prestige and value equated with the role of motherhood started with a long process of socialization back in 1760.

"Moralists, administrators, and doctors worked hard, presented their most subtle arguments to convince women to go back to their better feelings, and to breast feed once again..." It was the discourse of happiness and equality, a discourse that concerned them very much. For almost two centuries, ideologists promised them wonderful things were they to take up their motherly tasks. Be a good mother and you will be happy and well respected. Become indispensable within the family and you will achieve the rights of citizenship."

Roles that seem to truly belong to women (that is, the role of motherhood) have apparently been structured by men to benefit men because male society has manipulated women's psyches to accept motherhood according to the social purposes of the time, Badinter.

Women are also alienated, cornered, and confined by their maternal function, limited to being the instrument for the preservation of the species. It is the woman who must sacrifice her individual development in the name of that need. These observations by no means prove something negative about motherhood itself. Rather, they are a warning against the role of motherhood when it is imposed, alienating, neurotic, and/or compulsive.

In fact, how can the female sex only have two options for self-fulfillment as a woman: motherhood or the imitation of male roles? It is so very important to offer a third option for women—that is, the choice of free and conscious individual development.

It is important to repeat that what constitutes the most unique problem about motherhood is to be able to discern the mechanism within motherhood that directly hinders the evolution of humanity. Why do women have children? What is their true attitude toward motherhood? It is important to understand the original motivation for motherhood because, like any path, the initial impulse sets the foundation for its course.

In reality, no child is born free. In fact, a child comes into the world mortgaged or alienated to suit the mother's interests. To put it differently, children are not born to develop freely, but to satisfy the needs of their mothers, such as the following:

- A child is a way to receive love for free.
- A child fulfills the mother as a woman.
- A child makes a woman feel like a good person, that is to say, lovable and needed.
- A child fulfills the requirements for the image of an ideal mother; this role is in fact carried out for the image, and not for the mother's self.
- A child calms the anguish that comes from the castration complex (from the psychoanalytical standpoint, throughout pregnancy, women unconsciously feel they have recovered or received a penis).
- A child realizes the failed expectations of its parents.
- A child replaces a family member who has died, and to amend the parents' mistakes.
- A child constitutes the hope for protection and company in the mother's old age.

This phenomenon affects the world because new human beings only develop as a result of their mother's needs, which have been previously conditioned by the environment. The result is a vicious cycle that is impossible to break by ordinary means.

Understandably, progress for humanity is just not possible if each new generation is limited to repeating the neurotic preconceptions inherited from their mothers, who in turn inherited them from their respective mothers. The word neurotic has been used because of the compulsive mechanical aspect inherent in such preconceptions. This is especially true when mothers expect compensation from their children for all the things they have not been able to achieve in their lives.

Psychological coercion by the mother results in attitudes of rebellion, opposition, and hidden anger in the children. They cannot show these attitudes as they are mainly unconscious. Such aggressive attitudes towards the mother will later be displaced onto other people or directed inwards toward oneself.

A mother is omnipotent for the child from the prenatal age and throughout infancy. This engenders tremendous dependency, which later turns into rebellion. For boys, the insubordination of childhood translates into male chauvinism in adult life.

Motherly love is not as unselfish as believed because it can be used as a way to obtain prestige and recognition in order to fight the castration complex. Motherhood can also be used as a way to feel fulfilled as a woman through a glorified and universally accepted model.

What is so delicate about this whole matter is that women are the teachers of the world, since all men and women are under their direct care during infancy. This is especially true when the father has little time to spend with his children.

Is the female *Homo sapiens* able to guide her children when she has not even been able to develop herself?

It is clear that if a person does not fulfill oneself first, it is not possible to give anything to other people since logically one cannot give something one does not have.

The role of motherhood has been formed by tremendous social pressure directed at women so that they feel fulfilled exclusively through motherhood. Many women realize this only too late, when they are around forty or fifty and have several children, and are profoundly lonely.

The destiny of the world is in the hands of the female *Homo sapiens*, a being without an identity of her own, still copying male roles, seeking the realization of her own femininity exclusively through motherhood, without transcending the condition of being an erotic object.

This is one of the main reasons why civilization has not reached a higher level with regard to the humane quality of people. However, the day that women develop as individuals, reaching their maturity as human beings, there will be new hope for a better world because the highest human values will be fostered right from the crib. As long as women do not abandon frivolous and superficial attitudes, which prevent them from fulfilling their transcendental obligations, this vision will remain nothing more than a utopian dream.

Imagine the enormous push human progress could receive if mothers educated their children to satisfy the requirements of the world insofar as superior consciousness and morality are concerned, as opposed to educating them to fulfill their own needs. This would create a group of beings who possess social sensitivity and responsibility, and would be aware of the need to improve humanity. But for this, it would also be necessary for the educational system to be based on comprehension, not imposition. Parents are too accustomed to forcing their children to accept orders, rules, and regulations that they do not understand, as they usually do not explain the reasons behind their obligations; they simply make them obey.

It is of paramount importance that mothers stop forcing their own opinions and concepts onto their children, perpetuating their own schemes and flaws, and instead, give their children the freedom to be able to think for and develop by themselves. The mother's role as an educator must never be to make a psychological clone of themselves, but to create the proper conditions for care and nurturing so that the children will be able to find their own path of self-fulfillment and realization.

One can speak of true motherly love when the child is emotionally relinquished, not when it is used or managed as a tool for one's own lacks or ambitions. Relinquishing one's child emotionally does not indicate a lack of love; on the contrary, it constitutes a clean and superior love.

As was said before, *"new men and women develop only as a function of the mother's needs..."* Such needs are similar in most women, so it is important to remember them in the pursuit of consistency:

- Women unconsciously feel inferior to men due to the castration complex. This generates envy, aggression, and resentment as part of one's basic daily behavior.

- Women are exaggeratedly dependent on other people's opinions, and value themselves according to what other people reflect back to them.

- Women lack a psychic sexual identity, so they focus the realization of their femininity on the role of motherhood, on becoming erotic objects, or by imitating masculine roles.

- Women obsessively seek to fulfill their destiny through a relationship with a man instead of being self-referential. In this way, women become dependent on men, either copying them or fighting them.

- Women lack their own independent path for self-realization. Therefore, they need to fill themselves with things that have been created by men, for men, or against them.

- Women tend to see all other women as rivals. This tendency is rooted in a deep anger against their mothers whom they blame for not having made them whole. As a result, the young girl separates affectively from the mother, and turns all her interest toward the father, with the fantasy of obtaining a penis or child from him. At the same time, she has feelings of hostility and rivalry for her mother. Therefore, the first experience with the female gender is one of aversion. Later on, when she devotes herself to catching a man, she realizes that all women want to do the same, which means they are all her rivals.

- Women are driven by over identifying with their bodies, attempting to compensate for an inner emptiness with an obsessive care for their personal appearance. This is also used to satisfy female narcissism.
- Women often display frivolous and childish attitudes.
- Women are often obsessively preoccupied with other people's lives. This behavior is linked to the reliance on outside influences as discussed above in point 2. Whether through insecurity or lack of self-confidence, women look for models to copy and to reject. Of course, they copy the models that coincide with their own guidelines, no matter how bad they may be, and reject the ones that do not coincide with their ideas, even if they would be perfect or useful for them.
- Women are more anguished and anxious than men.
- Women are unhappier, more frustrated, and more bitter than men.
- Women are exaggeratedly concerned with social recognition.
- Women have a tendency to negatively exploit their own passivity and use it as a means to control other people.
- Women have a compulsive fear of abandonment. This can have pathologic repercussions if it occurs.
- Women seem to lack self-confidence which makes them more emotionally vulnerable.
- Women are driven to be valued as a woman, not as an individual person.
- Women tend to make their decisions based on their likes or dislikes.
- Women often use venomous language. This is a manifestation of female aggression and is a hidden way of using language to wound or to attack without it being apparent.

All these impulses share an interesting common denominator: passion. This is a woman's first erroneous behavior. Remember that the word *passion* comes from *passive* meaning passive behavior, not active behavior with respect to one's "I." Thus, women tend not to have a mature, adult, strong, and developed "I." Instead, they have a female "I," which rules those aspects of their nature that have to do with being an erotic object.

There are many examples in which women use their children as tools for their own passionate behavior. Here are some examples:

- When a woman wishes to get pregnant in order to keep the father of the child
- When a woman uses her children as hostages to pressure the husband to behave the way she wants
- When, after a couple has separated, the woman urges the children to go against their father, passing on to them her own resentment and frustration, using them as a means to pressure him
- When a woman uses her children so that others will feel pity for her, or to get help from others
- When she teaches them to hate the same way she hates

In addition, many women desire maternity in order to fulfill their own needs, not to give. The entire sacrifice of pregnancy, childbirth, the child's rearing and sustenance, are alienated from its genesis and development. In fact, the entire effort is ultimately directed toward the mother herself because the child is most often a tool that the mother uses unconsciously to satisfy her own needs.

When this happens, childbirth does not represent the ultimate unselfish act of giving life, but rather the anxious proof of a woman's femininity whose purpose is not to conceive, carry, and give birth to a new being so that it finds its own destiny, but rather, to unite this new being to her own destiny and to calm her unsatisfied anxieties. That is the reason why newborn boys and girls are only able to develop within the narrow spectrum of neurotic limitations imposed on them by their mothers; limitations that serve the mother's passionate behavior, which comes to represent guidelines for their own learning about humanity. Therefore, new generations are basically no better than old ones; they merely appear to be different, not more developed.

A new generation only represents a different psychological program implemented by combining social learning with the mother's instruction. It does not contemplate de-programming, or the possibility to condition oneself according to one's own desires, considerations, and individual ideas.

Permissive education, which is based on letting the child do as it wishes, also represents a movement against the parents because the basic drive behind it is to value all that is contrary or different from parental guidelines. It does not take into consideration the authentic possibility of being able to choose because it is compulsive.

The alternative to permissive education would be a system which obliges children to think. They would then be able to choose for themselves and become responsible for their actions.

As stated previously, the maternal instinct does not exist automatically. This might make many women feel devalued, believing that they have scant feminine sensitivity and that this concept might be denying them a higher quality that is essential for women. The opposite is true: this concept offers a great advantage because it represents the difference between animal and human reproduction.

Animal instinct obliges the various species to raise their young in the same way. All eagles, for example, educate their chicks in the same way, without making any distinction among them. They have done so in the same manner since the beginning of time and will continue to do so indefinitely. That is why an animal's characteristics remain fixed; animals do not experience progress with regard to evolving into higher forms of life. (Time here is measured according to human chronology.)

If it is true that the female *Homo sapiens* lacks an authentic and automatic maternal instinct, she has the possibility to conceive and raise beings in a freer manner, since she would not be tied to a rigid model. This offers two principle advantages:

1. Freedom to choose whether or not to be a mother
2. Freedom to decide what kind of mother she will be, according to the needs of her children

I believe it is very important for women to realize the great advantages of not having a ready-made maternal instinct because instincts produce repetitive uniformity, whereas, if adequately prepared, a human being can create ways to higher development and be more selective regarding one's child's education. This means that an individual recipe for each child can exist while instinct implies all creatures of the same species share the same recipe.

Of course, to be able to provide individual education, the mother also needs to have been educated in the same way or to have developed herself according to the guidelines presented in this book. A woman who was brought up and trained instinctively by the same guidelines for everyone will not be able to use her own intelligence adequately for what has been proposed here.

Even though the maternal instinct does not exist, it has been replaced by something else: the human cultural program. Unfortunately, this also leads to uniformity and dictates collective formulas for education and upbringing.

When mothers take courses on how to raise their children, the only thing they learn is one system applied uniformly to all their children. The system varies only according to the model of the mother's cultural upbringing and birthplace.

Natural instinct has been replaced by cultural programming, but with very few advantages. The result is corrupt behavior that was once pure in its origin because it sought to fulfill the human being's essential and most basic obligation: *striving to elevate consciousness to its highest level.* The unfortunate failure in the system consists of the fact that cultural programming concentrates instead on developing intelligence, which is a faculty of the nervous system. Without the direction of a superior, adult, and mature "I," intelligence is merely an erratic and unpredictable ability. Without the guidance of a superior "I," even if one's intelligence has been developed, it is not certain that it will be used toward helping social evolution, or to forming the individual's inner world, which is key to the evolution of mankind's inner nature.

A mother, who is truly self-realized as a woman, should establish a dynamic relationship with her child and be sufficiently flexible to satisfy the child's individual needs. When a general recipe for child-rearing is followed, what happens? Picture the educational results of an authoritarian mother who is trying to teach a shy child. Without a doubt, the mother will end up drowning the child on a psychic level, frustrating its personal initiative and impulse toward development. Now picture the same authoritarian mother and a willful and rebellious child. The entire relationship will be marked with unproductive conflicts. Finally, picture the same rebellious child with a timid, indecisive and fragile mother.

Repetitive behavior that stems from the instincts or from cultural programming does not bring about progress within the inner nature of people. Instead, it hinders the evolution of mankind. Repetitive behavior is static. It is not dynamic. It is has more in common with death than with life.

Therein resides one of the keys for feminine realization. The first requirement for starting one's transformation is to understand one's mechanical and repetitive behavior, and how such behavior halts the evolution of a woman. It is imperative to be convinced that, in order to change and progress, it is necessary to break away from habitual forms of behavior. Otherwise, one will remain stagnant and passive, bonded to inertia and entropy.

The main characteristic of an alienated being is an annulled capacity for change and transformation which condemns the subject to a state of suspended animation or psychic catalepsy. Unless one can awaken from this profound stupor, no evolution will be possible.

Sadly, each child that is born into this world arrives shackled to its mother's psychological needs. Its destiny is mortgaged, contaminated, manipulated by human passions, and is without genuine freedom of choice. Even more grievous, the child comes into life in order to fulfill the mother's neurotic needs.

The next time one is overwhelmed with feelings of protection and fuzziness for a newborn, whether of a neighbor, friend, or woman passing by, one should not forget that the child has not been born free, but rather, is chained to the mother's condition. Until women truly develop themselves as individuals, there is little hope for a better world.

Could it be that women do not have a real interest in becoming emancipated from men by attaining higher individual aspirations? Do they instead want to perpetuate their current situation of helplessness and psychological vulnerability? Certainly, if women do not work toward their evolution, they will be more and more dependent on men, more and more masculine, less a person and more a thing, and will thus continue to raise their children in a manner that completely destroys the possibilities for evolution and for the survival of humanity.

Remember that only a self-realized individual will be able to give. The decision to continue being one more female or to develop into an authentic woman is in the hands of the female gender. As authentic women, they can then aspire to become the *teachers of the world*, a possibility that is higher than the role of motherhood and transcends the purely physical. To become authentic, it is first necessary to sublimate the part of the personality that is selfish, savage, greedy, irresponsible and criminal, because this behavior belongs to the primitive and unconscious part of the human being. If not, one will be absolutely incapable of helping one's children sublimate the same primitive, archaic force.

An overwhelming majority of women do not have the ability or the knowledge to help their own children fulfill their individual potential and become self-realized according to each child's own needs. And, on the subject of self-realization, it is imperative that it include an interest for the evolution of society.

# SEXUAL BALANCE

As with many other aspects, women are subject to two contradictory forces regarding sexual satisfaction. On the one hand, they are told repeatedly that sex is sinful, while simultaneously feeling the natural impulse to express erotic desire. It is easy to see how cornered a woman might feel faced with these two contradictory forces. Hence, a great deal of nervous or psychosomatic disorders stem from the repression of their libidos. If a woman engages in sexual activities similar to those of men, she might be called a whore or sinner. If she represses this force, she can become frustrated and bitter.

In comparison to men, women are considerably more frustrated and dissatisfied, sexually speaking. Even though its importance is controversial, frigidity is a disorder that affects a large part of the female population. Experts employ different criteria to evaluate the percentage of frigid women. Alfred Kinsey stated that only ten percent of women are truly frigid. Edmund Bergler, a former lecturer at the New York Psychoanalytic Institute and assistant director of the Vienna Psychoanalytic Clinic, said that, "frigidity is a problem that affects seventy to eighty percent of all women." Other researchers indicate ranges somewhere in between these two extremes.

If frigidity is thought of as the difficulty or impossibility to experience orgasm, it is obvious then that a majority of women are affected by it. If frigidity is defined by the impossibility to enjoy sex, that is, to experience pleasure even though orgasm is not reached, clearly that percentage drops somewhat.

Nevertheless, it is clear that women have not been able to find an adequate channel for sexual expression, one that will permit them to enjoy sex in a balanced way without repressing or letting their instincts run unrestrained.

Looking at the sexual behavior of women throughout history, one can see that it has fluctuated constantly between acting without moral restraint and Puritanism. Men, on the other hand, have always acted in a manner that has not changed much. Currently, women fall into four groups:

1. Women who are totally repressed, and who do not enjoy sex at all.

2. Those who enjoy sex, but do not reach orgasm, or only reach it occasionally.

3. Those who enjoy a satisfactory relationship and reach orgasm regularly.

4. Those who, in search of liberation, confuse sex with indiscriminate sexual freedom, trying to prove that they can have sex and reach orgasm as easily as eating a piece of cake, or drinking a cup of coffee. The only criterion is for the man to be somewhat decent.

The women in the last group have gone to the extreme of imitating men's genital activity because they have done away with the essence of the feminine sexual response: emotional participation which acts through the limbic system to initiate sexual excitement in women.

The first group is especially interesting. In my view repression does not do away with enjoyment; it just perverts it. In fact, nothing has hurt the female gender more than the story of original sin which states that sex is a mortal sin because women have done something expressly prohibited by the Creator. Due to original sin, they were punished with expulsion from Paradise. This story has been widely disseminated by educators and moralists who have implanted a basic message in people's minds: "sex is sinful and dirty." Unfortunately, this affects women almost exclusively since the majority of men have never been socialized to restrict their sexual activity. Furthermore, Eve is seen as having more guilt in the original sin, since it was she who was incited by the snake to make Adam sin. As mentioned before, that is why women were considered the embodiment of evil in ancient times.

Women have been socialized to restrict their sexuality. They have been told, directly or covertly, that sex is dishonest and impure and that to be a good woman, this energy must be repressed until marriage. (This also explains the neurotic or compulsive need for wanting to get married—to get permission to have sex without it being a sin.)

Unfortunately, the idea of original sin is much stronger in the unconscious of women than the idea of sexual freedom through marriage. So, even when married, there are hidden obstacles that hinder enjoyment of sex.

This moralist message needs to be modified in content and in form of transmission otherwise its effects may be the exact opposite of what was intended. Even an amateur behavioral psychologist, as well as those who have heard of Pavlov and Skinner, will understand that with respect to this subject women are being clearly conditioned and recorded with an unconscious association between sexuality and sin. Women are being programmed to respond sexually only in sinful situations and to remain unresponsive in regular or harmless situations such as in a legal marriage.

This is not the first case where science has backfired. History is full of similar painful examples. Their explanations lie in the tremendous gap between scientific development and the expansion of human consciousness. Human beings can be trained to become progressively more intelligent, but this capacity must be to serve a higher consciousness.

The above explains certain female behavior that cannot be understood in any other way. The behavior I am referring to has to do with women who can only reach orgasm with a lover but not with their husbands. A simple explanation could be that the lover is more considerate, caring, and loving than the husband, but this is often not the case. Usually, the opposite is true.

There are many documented cases of women with model husbands who do not have any problems with their virility, but nonetheless, they cannot reach orgasm with them. However, they seem to have no difficulty with an inconsiderate or even perverted lover with whom they have purely animalistic relationships. In fact, they are able to reach the pinnacle of pleasure.

The explanation is clear—the lover symbolizes something sinful and since sex had been previously associated with sin, it represents the only possible way to liberate that sexual force. In this case, conditioning by association is like permission to let go sexually and since the husband does not represent sin but rather virtue the woman's libido is repressed and its expression is held back.

This helps to understand why some women can only have sex with men who are low-life's, violent or beasts, who treat them as disposable objects, humiliating and punishing them. Frequently, the more bestial a man is the more sinful he appears and the easier it is for some women to give free rein to their sexual responses.

How many women fall head over heels in love with men who are immoral, criminals, sadists or pimps? In fact, aggressive men with bad reputations tend to be very successful with the female gender. This is especially true in the case of insecure adolescents who find a way to expiate their sexual guilt by receiving emotional mistreatment.

The situations that trigger different erotic responses in women are related to what each woman considers sinful. If a woman associates dishonesty with having sex with married men, this is how she will be able to enjoy sex. If another woman thinks it is sinful to be with men who are considerably older than she is, an older man will be able to make her react easily.

This refers specifically to women who are more affected by the mechanism that associates sexuality with sin, since other women will most likely react according to different intensities and criteria.

Even though this discussion has focused principally on the first group, even the third group is not free from this conditioning. Many women in the third group also engage in masochistic or obscene fantasies in order to reach orgasm. This book has already shown sadomasochism as inadequate behavior in woman.

It would be really valuable to implement educational systems that foster morals born from reflection rather than from imposition, in other words, values chosen freely and consciously by each individual person, without being imitated or forced.

When a woman's libido is repressed, she will tend to be more vulnerable to erotic incitement than a man because she has been taught to repress her libidinous impulses from an early age. In time she will have accumulated an extremely potent sensual charge which, like a time bomb, becomes very sensitive to the correct trigger.

When women go to see a strip-tease show, they can be considerably more audacious and less inhibited than men in similar situations.

Voracity in the female gender is manifested when women indulge in malicious gossip about frivolous events in the lives of others, their work companions, or about women belonging to some other group. When discussing as hearsay, for example, about the sexual adventures of another woman, the erotic fuse of those women participating in the gossip is immediately lit, and their criticism or comments about the woman in question's behavior can be surprisingly incisive, obscene, and aggressive. They are unaware that they are really expressing their unconscious envy for not being the ones who had caught the prey.

It seems that envy is a prominent characteristic in ordinary women, women who not only feel resentful toward men, but also feel intense rivalry and antagonism toward the same sex with whom they compete for male admiration.

Further evidence of the intense repressed aggression that exists in the female libido is apparent when a woman feels jealousy or spite. Feeling thus, she might burst into obscenities and rudeness against the man who provoked her.

There is a moral, rather than scientific, explanation for such unpleasant female behavior. Such mistaken behaviors stem from repression of the libido, which can become like a stagnant pond of water that receives neither air nor oxygen and is decomposing and losing its natural qualities.

The problem for most women is that they have not found their sexual balance and easily enter into a state of imbalance which makes them waiver between guilt and frustration.

The solution to this conflict cannot be found in an external formula or recipe, nor can it be attained by imitating others or by following ignorant advice or strict guidelines. It must be born out of individual freedom based on the deliberate development of oneself.

Some individuals are free and others are still vassals. Unfortunately, there are too few of the former. Free individuals have somehow acquired the power to responsibly decide their actions, take charge of their lives, accumulate meaningful experiences, learn to reconcile personal and social interests without relying on other people's opinions, and value themselves for their inner achievements, not external ones. In other words, they have become mature and adult enough to determine to a certain extent the thread of their own destiny.

Women have within all the tools with which they need to create themselves and to develop transcendental values that will allow them to have uninterrupted inner growth. If a woman is convinced that she possesses these values, she will know that she is able to solve any problem she may face, and that she does not need to depend on a man to solve her problems. She must, once and for all, understand the absolute need to become psychologically independent from men and to create her own individual role as a woman.

The negative concept of sex is a very outdated one and it is time to stress the opposite: that is, the adoration or glorification of libidinous energy as a nonspecific universal power of creation whose direction does not depend on its own impulse, but on the direction given to it by human beings. The art of sublimation of the libido has everything to do with this concept of the human being directing libidinous energy. We can understand it better by analyzing the opposite concept of corruption. Corruption begins when individuals contaminate their imaginations and their hearts with hatred, aggression, lust, concupiscence, or pornography. The contamination, that is, the corrupt waste coming from one's imagination and feelings, spills over into the unspecified flow of libidinous energy, rupturing a person's inner balance and disturbing the healthy flow of libidinous energy.

It is often said that sin lies within a person. In fact, a corrupt intention contaminates and takes the virtue out of an action that might be outwardly correct.

Sublimation of the feminine libido must be based on adequate hygiene of the imagination whose purity reflects an equivalent inner attitude of cleansing and ordering one's internal world. In this way sublimation acts as a compass for this libidinous force, since it is nonspecific in its intrinsic nature; it simply adapts to the vital mandate issued from a person's inner disposition.

A repressed libido expresses the force of *Thanatos*, and is like a pond of stagnant water that decomposes since it has no oxygen. A river that flows fluidly represents *Eros*, conversely, in all of its vital potential.

When something is repressed, it is as if it has been entombed, buried and hidden in the attic of the unconscious. Sublimation, on the other hand, occurs when that thing is brought into the light and confronted consciously and responsibly.

It is important to remember that repression is a process by which impulses that originate in the Id are repeated cyclically; they are not extinguished but restrained and restricted. Because their original potency remains intact, a great amount of psychic energy is needed to keep them at bay. Although primitive and unconscious, these impulses constitute a force of unimagined energy.

Sublimation, therefore, means to raise energy that normally circulates at a lower level to a higher channel. This is where the precise difference between the conscious and the unconscious is found. The unconscious represents the underground part of the mind, whereas the conscious part can be seen on the surface.

The alienation that women experience when their lives are centered around a man represents a total loss of self-control because they are controlled by external forces that take hold of their minds and make them behave alienated or differently from how they should. In a deeper sense this means that when a woman is controlled by external forces, her "I" is obliterated and replaced by a possessive or alienated "I." This alienated "I" is comprised of influences from the paternalistic society as well as from biological factors that have not really been understood, such as the so-called lacking due to the absence of a penis.

Just as the individual psyche, according to Jung, is an appendage of the collective unconscious, a woman will remain an appendage of a man for as long as she has not achieved psychological individuality.

Obviously, there is only one way to oppose the influence of alien forces that control or direct one's mind, and that is through self-control.

This is achieved through reflective consciousness, which generates its own energy to resist the penetration of all alien forces. The manipulation of one's own conscience is only possible after one has realized that such alien forces do not belong to the individual and that they invade and control one's behavior.

The goal in the process of resistance is to form an "I" with enough power and permanence to ensure mental autonomy.

From the point of view of self-control, men generally seem to have a significant advantage over women because their sense of obligation and the responsibilities of their social role as men require them to be more disciplined in life in order to be successful.

On the other hand, the female gender more often plays at living, without truly facing life, as if everything she does were something temporary, like a pre-matrimonial, pre-maternal, or pre-old-age activity. It seems that when a woman has a profession or certain skill, it is only to serve as life insurance in case marriage does not save her, but not an activity for the rest of her life. Female socialization emphasizes passivity and weakness. These characteristics are just the opposite of the strength required for self-discipline or self-control.

Instead of becoming strong, the female prefers to play the part of being weak with the sole purpose and goal of finding a male to protect her. If she does not find a man, all of her existence is considered a waste, since the path of passive weakness means that she gave up development and self-realization. But if she finds a man, her destiny would not change because her dependence would prevent her from self-development. However, if she chooses the path of self-growth she would not need to submit to a man in order to do so.

This model of femininity reconciles strength with beauty into one being. I believe that women can be simultaneously strong and intensely feminine but their strength must be based on true femininity and not on the concept of strength that men exhibit.

A man's strength is made up of the following elements:

- Muscular strength
- A greater capacity for aggression because of male hormones
- The penetrating nature of his virile constitution; an energy that makes him conquer, achieve, explore, and seek out many different activities
- Willpower with respect to the capacity to sustain arduous efforts, which is what in turn gives them the ability to achieve

Thus, a man's strength is muscular, hormonal, libidinous, and willful.

What do women usually do when they compete with men? They imitate male roles in order to excel using the same techniques men use.

Women extract strength from the following factors:

- By becoming emotionally aggressive to artificially raise their levels of testosterone. This gives them a greater capacity for aggression, but makes them more masculine.
- By counterattacking or substituting male muscular strength with the force of passive aggressiveness by:
  o Using words that are as sharp as a knife, words that hurt, disqualify, insult, ridicule, despise, and offend through covert messages.
  o Using passivity as a means to manipulate other people so they will do what she wants, using passive-aggressive mechanisms to manipulate and control.
- Personal rejection by means of a cold and obstinate attitude.
- Emotional selfishness and indifference.
- Exaggeratedly authoritarian, manifested as a neurotic need for control and a lack of flexibility.

Women who try to beat male robustness through the power of disguised aggression become psychically more masculine. By using the same kind of energy, it is as if they were fighting darkness by creating more darkness. In this case, one cannot speak of complementary opposites because such women either become actively masculine or inwardly passive.

Why not employ *active passiveness*?

There are two types of passiveness; one is inert and the other active. This can be proven by practicing relaxation techniques diligently. One of the following two things will happen—either one will fall asleep and the body will relax, or the body becomes passive, but the activity of one's thoughts notably increases.

Take, for example, the ancient Eastern symbol of YIN and YANG. The clear portion of the diagram below represents masculinity (YANG) and the dark part represents femininity (YIN). We could say that when females want to be equal to males they do so by fighting YANG with YANG.

It would be more natural to use the power of YIN that naturally corresponds to a woman.

This type of force is similar to a reed in a storm. In order to withstand the force of the storm it must be flexible and bend instead of breaking. A great oak tree, on the other hand, would not be able to resist the force of a storm and would fall. Yielding can sometimes be more productive than standing rigidly still.

Women must develop the strength that resides in their passiveness by mobilizing an inner energy conceived from within. She must be able to accomplish this while preserving her intrinsically feminine quality of *inner receptiveness*, by abandoning attempts to compete with men, and focusing instead on the fulfillment of her own potential, independently of what that potential represents to men.

When a woman understands the immense power for transformation that her uterus represents, she will see that the capacity to envelop and surround is as strong, if not stronger, than muscular strength or hormonal aggressiveness. What males achieve through the strength of aggressive force, women can obtain through a softness that is firm in its receptivity and ability to surround and persuade. Such harmonious ways of being form a feminine identity equal in its representation of strength. By doing so, women will make full use of the psychic capacities of their feminine reproductive systems. The vagina and the uterus are therefore not passive and inert cavities. Within them resides prodigious latent activity that is ready to be mobilized at the precise moment that conception is required.

Women who work with a majority of men have sometimes commented on how difficult it can be to relate to male colleagues who treat them as just another male, not giving them the respect they deserve. In order to get respect, they might increase their aggressiveness and authoritarian attitudes and become openly hostile. By employing male force, their situation gets worse because they become more masculine. If they get respect under these circumstances, it is as a male, not as a female.

When a woman develops a reflective conscience and a capacity for self-control, she will quickly understand that she can inspire respect far better by highlighting her feminine qualities of receptivity, softness, sweetness, and envelopment. This is how to gain equality with men.

Evidence of this strength was apparent when Gandhi forced the British to leave India by using YIN energy against YANG.

Women need to create within themselves, within their psychic uteruses, a force that will remain unchangeable in its intrinsic constitution. This must be done through reflective consciousness. Women need to calmly meditate on the fact that the penis and uterus are opposites and complementary and that neither is superior in its capacities. This has to do with psychosomatic integrity, that is, considering each organ according to its biological and psychic aspects.

Women must understand that their conceiving force is as valuable and powerful as masculine creativity, and that they have no reason to feel diminished in their self-esteem. Of course, it is essential to utilize such inner vision and convert it into an authentically adult and autonomous form of behavior, independent from the influence of men. *Women need to become seekers and finders of their own individual feminine paths.* By building up a repertoire of these experiences, a woman will be able to develop a very high level of self-confidence and self-esteem.

Yet, as has been said before in this book, there is still a powerful obstacle that stands in the way. It has to do with the comfortable attitude of dependency, of not making decisions or working too hard, of being only minimally responsible for one's own actions. This behavior can hold a woman back from freeing herself from the alienation that ails her, choosing instead to remain in a comfortable space, albeit unproductive and limited, of dependence on men. A woman who accepts such conditions needs to recognize that she has accepted with her eyes wide open to be discriminated against, and that she has stunted her possibility for development, and cannot blame anyone but herself for these circumstances.

The feminine model just described above is not arbitrary; it is based on the capacities bestowed on women by nature, and is about expressing and using what is legitimately within them. It does not constitute an artificially contrived model that is imposed by force. Therefore, the proposed model is not a mere recommendation, a method for success, or some sort of gracious advice. It is a most severe warning for women to open their eyes and behold the evidence that is buried internally, underneath layers of social mandates and complete apathy. Self-realization does not require the kind of willpower that is used to force or impose something; rather, it has to do with inner openness toward one's very own essence.

All women need to choose between acting falsely as caricatures of what they are, or surrendering within themselves to the natural archetype of the eternal feminine, which has not been manifested as such in humanity's history.

A woman's authentic femininity can be found in the following actions and attitudes:

- To free oneself through reflective consciousness from the concept of sex as sin, and understand that the libido is a nonspecific energy that obeys human behavior.

- To value sexuality as equal to men; to understand that both men and women possess psychic and biological capacities of equal value.

- To develop one's "I" with goals that are not made for men or by men, but that represent the woman's path of individual self-realization.

- To completely renounce competing with men since it is not necessary to prove equality by combating or despising men. Women need only concentrate on fostering their own growth.

- To acquire sufficient maturity and self-confidence to find one's own criteria, inner judgment, responsibility and correct sexual homeostasis, so as to allow complete and authentic sexual satisfaction.

- To practice imaginative and emotional hygiene; to become aware that destructive ideas and aggressive feelings contaminate the libido. (When one develops a harmonious and balanced "I," negative forces lose strength.)

- To understand that the real strength of women lies in their wise use of the YIN principle—which is the complementary opposite to YANG or masculine energy; to understand that the essence of femininity lies in being flexible, agile, active, and transforming in the act of receptivity, sweet, soft, enveloping, and coaxing.

- To be able to regulate interpersonal relationships wisely, considering that other people have feelings and ideas that should be respected, and that their expectations and rights are as legitimate as one's own. This attitude comes from constantly practicing empathy, learning to place oneself emotionally in another's shoes.

- To choose to become emancipated from men's guardianship; to renounce being an eternal protégée of men; to understand that a woman has a tremendous internal capacity to engender her own path in life, to fulfill her own desires and forge a prosperous and happy destiny.

- To give up all attempts at using men as a means to fulfill one's own plans.

# DEVELOPMENT

What is the starting point for a woman who wishes to develop as an individual?

She will need to become aware of her real situation, and that by virtue of being born female, she was born facing a specific conflict: having to choose between the preservation of the species or her individual development. For all the reasons posited thus far, it would seem that social circumstances deprive women of many possibilities for development, directing a large part of their life force toward reproduction.

Are these two options contradictory?

A sustained reflection about this dilemma will make evident that when the role of motherhood is compulsive, it castrates a woman with regard to her individual fulfillment. However, if a woman chooses the role of motherhood from her own free will, that act can become an instrument of union between social and individual evolution. One must only order the options correctly: individual development needs to precede motherhood because in order to be a mother, one can only give what one has, and to have something to give means that first one has to have oneself. In other words, only when a woman is fulfilled can she decide if she wishes to be a mother, when and how to do so, and how to educate the child in the correct manner.

Motherhood does not imply femininity. One can test this theory out by comparing the attitudes of mature women with regard to their children. Are they still as anxious as they were during the period prior to having their children when they hoped the children would make them more of a woman? Or did they simply become more female?

It would be useful for women to realize how small the world of the female is (as opposed to that of a woman). In fact, in the female world, which is so restricted and small, women are confined to being attractive, to catching a man, and to having children. Such goals, attitudes, and external props are not constructive for them at all: wanting to be attractive only for men, having children merely to satisfy the social role, catching a man in order to live psychically through him. It is obvious that these attitudes are not at all useful for them and merely offer compensation for feelings of inferiority and feelings of weakness.

If women choose to be merely females they will have chosen a path of permanent slavery with no possibility to direct their own destinies because the energy that could be used for their own development is used to take care of their physical appearance, to catch a man, or to foment in themselves narcissistic mechanisms that will influence their psychological needs.

This is similar to being a worker bee when one could become a queen bee. There is a kind of royal jelly through which a woman can grow and transform into becoming queen of her inner world, becoming a fully developed feminine person. The food in question is formed when a woman consciously processes everyday experiences within her psychic uterus, that is, within her inner world that constitutes the dwelling place of her "I." A woman's psychic uterus is a transcendental space that marks the difference between being an object or a subject, between inanimate matter and a conscious being. However, the task at hand requires a substantial change of attitude regarding everyday interests, since she will need to redirect the energy that she uses toward keeping up her personal appearance and perennial competition and comparison with men inwardly. Her choice will be to develop transcendental values, not external ones.

What is known is that external values gradually dwindle with the passing of time because they are linked to the body, which inevitably deteriorates. When one uses material goods to bolster oneself and to raise one's self-esteem, identifying with the prestige and power represented by them, one is definitely hindering the development of one's "I," which gets separated from the individual. Material goods also represent a false security because their so-called benefits are not located within the person, but within the person's possessions.

Evolution must be based on a dynamic interaction between subject and environment. However, when an individual lives projected toward the outside, constantly merging with it, this life force is annulled. This is exactly what occurs when one spends one's life waiting for external events, objects, or people to change or modify one's life from the outside, rendering real individual action impossible.

An object does not relate to the environment dynamically; instead, it remains passively at the environment's disposal, willing to be modeled according to the whim of external events. Such an object is used by the environment and has no possibility to do anything useful for itself.

Women who accept to be objects are available to men, but not to themselves. Feminists might believe they do not fit this category, but if they take men as their reference points, then their actions, too, are conditioned by men, and it is as if they were living for them.

To become an object means to close oneself to life, to remain inert, or petrified; it denotes an inability to receive or give creatively.

The female sex also urgently requires a broader perspective to enable women to differentiate between trivial and transcendental things and to prioritize attention and actions toward the latter. Unfortunately, more often than not, women get absorbed in utterly puerile or petty matters, ascribing to them a sense of importance and priority, while neglecting what is truly valuable. This is how women forget the thread that holds together their lives: they run after a new dress to wear to a special event, or talk about the most recent romance of movie stars. In these circumstances women either lack the ability to reflect upon what is of vital importance or they lack the ability to face reality, and prefer to evade it through self-deceiving tactics. Often, desperately urgent and important matters are dealt with frivolously or superficially, as if denying the danger is preferable.

A broader perspective permits one to rise above temporary circumstances and to discern levels of importance and urgency in order to set priorities. It is essential therefore to train oneself to have perfect mental clarity, which is absolutely necessary to develop a reliable orientation system. This role is carried out by thought. If our minds were perturbed, neither money nor material power would help us achieve our goals. A person cannot extract anything positive from his or her existence if that person is psychically petrified, or unable to assertively make changes or progress with regard to his or her evolution.

Of course, the human being's most urgent priority is to be alive because with death all possibilities for self-fulfillment become null. However, to be alive does not mean to exist only on the physical plane; it means to take possession of one's individual existence together with the ability to determine one's own destiny in a fairly autonomous manner. When one is a mere object at the mercy of the vicissitudes of circumstances one really lacks an individual life and is only animated by the force that emanates from the social entity.

When a woman becomes convinced of the need to make her individual evolution a priority, and after she has truly understood the essence of the concepts in this book, she must dedicate her efforts and exercises toward her individual development in order to become conscious of her inner world.

## *BECOMING CONSCIOUS OF ONE'S INNER WORLD*

The inner world is comprised of desires, thoughts, emotions, fears, fantasies, and everything else that a person feels. These reactions are mostly unconscious, without the individual realizing what is happening within. Therefore, the person is unable to realize what motivates his or her behavior, or understand the impact and significance of many daily events.

The average person does not manage his or her inner world, but rather is managed by it, thus losing the possibility to choose.

For a woman to create her own psychic uterus, she must become conscious of what is happening in her inner world, constantly observe and question it; ask herself at all times, the why and what of everything. She must do this work daily, since it is like discovering the vein of a previously ignored inner gold mine. People often find it hard to see the obvious, and they appreciate least what is close to them. A woman's work therefore has to do with exploring herself in order to discover and know the elements that lie within, which are like valuable minerals waiting to be discovered. Nevertheless, precious metals are never found in a pure state; they are mixed with other elements of little value, with waste material. It is thus necessary to effectively sublimate and separate what is valuable from what serves no purpose. This process is carried out by knowing, realizing, becoming aware, noticing, enlightening, and becoming conscious of all the dark zones of the soul by paying attention to what is happening inside.

All that is perceived must be put into words because language has order, structure, and hierarchy. This is the process by which unconscious impulses are brought up to the level of intelligence.

One should keep a diary and write down the results of one's analysis. One should avoid moral judgments about one's own fantasies, and concentrate instead on just writing down the experiences as they occur.

The next step is to learn how to communicate everything that one has learned to a person one trusts, letting that person know what one comes to know about oneself and discussing the significance of each example.

The three phases, that is, becoming conscious, putting examples into words, and communicating the examples, must take place gradually and all three steps must be completed. They must be carried out in the order described and one must not jump to the following phase until each phase has received full attention. This practice must be done continuously throughout one's life. This is how one can give conscious form to the content of one's unconscious, sublimating and releasing its latent capacities.

It is foolish to believe that the exploration of the inner world will be a miraculous panacea because the results of such processes can only be evaluated over time. At first, there will probably be pain, anguish, disorientation, loneliness, and fear. However, by confronting these experiences and by starting to manage what was once out of one's control, one will gradually reach calm, peace, tranquility, and self-confidence. One might achieve temporary calm by evading certain realities, but such avoidance will eventually give rise to increased anguish because of the uncertainty that surrounds unresolved conflicts.

Even though many questions will surface as one starts to become conscious of inner events, one should not feel compelled to answer them all right away. The answers, as well as the results of one's work, will present themselves gradually over time, little by little, and can only be analyzed once completely revealed. Therefore, it is important not to try and force answers because otherwise one will cut the spontaneity with which they surface. The goal is not to have answers. It is the journey toward the answers that is important.

Emotional problems can quite often destroy people since people become desperate because they do not understand what is really happening to them. Conflicts stem from the inability to reconcile opposing impulses. These opposing impulses are not born from one's intelligence and they are only instinctive pulses struggling mechanically to achieve some goal. A good example of this has to do with love and hate. These opposites can exist quite perfectly at the same time within a person. For example, when a child feels love and hate toward his parents at the same time a profound unease and anguish is produced. When a child is able to understand that it is normal to feel anger against parents, who themselves feel anger as well, and that what is important is not whether one feels aggression or not but how it is managed and what is done with it, then the child can reconcile these opposites and feel at peace.

Often the individual expects too much from other people and demands things that he or she would never demand from him or herself. When such exaggerated, capricious, and artificial expectations are not fulfilled, the person might feel disillusioned or bitter, not because others have failed, but because the individual was unable to use them as instruments for his or her own pleasure.

When one fails at manipulating others, the result is always depression, but more often than not, the person does not recognize his or her own failure and blames others.

When a woman has trained herself to observe what happens internally, she will learn to achieve greater control over her conflicts, since she will have removed from them the non-reflective component.

Through reflection and by adding awareness to them, they will no longer be reactive.

It is therefore very important for women to slowly but surely observe what is happening within themselves, carefully scrutinizing what they are feeling and why. By adopting this method, women will be able to give meaning to impulses that were previously unintelligible and unconscious. This is in line with the highest form of human development, which is to become the master of oneself as one develops full consciousness. This capacity is formed gradually by learning about one's inner world. Such knowledge is like royal jelly that will allow the gradual growth and development of the "I."

Many people, and especially women, live waiting for spectacular events to happen and scorn common and everyday events, thus limiting their possibilities for change. Such individuals do not reap the meaningful lessons of life or partake in the strength that can be obtained through everyday experiences that have been processed within. By focusing expectations on big events that more often than not do not even take place, people waste a great deal of their lives. It is essential to understand that the richness of life does not lie in the events themselves, but in how a person makes use of them (or are used by them) to increase one's consciousness. A common event is an element that can destroy or build one up. For women, common events can represent tedium and internal deterioration or an opportunity to create royal jelly through which they will be transformed into queens. Each and every day is another opportunity to create, grow, and become self-realized, not to be spent in games and silly pastimes.

Perhaps it will be useful for me to offer some guidelines regarding how one can become aware of one's inner world. Please be forewarned, however, that these guidelines do not represent a method of self-analysis since my intention is to provide only a general idea to individuals who have little or no practice in observing their inner worlds.

There is no complete answer to the question about what one needs to observe because in reality every manifestation of one's inner world merits observation.

## GUIDELINES FOR DEVELOPING AWARENESS OF ONE'S INNER WORLD:

- Describe what usually makes you angry or aggressive and give details about the mechanisms involved.
- What makes you happy? Why?

- What makes you sad? Why?
- What makes you feel important? Why?
- What makes you feel depressed? Why?
- What humiliates you? Why?
- What makes you excited? Why?
- What have you felt or do you feel when you fall in love?
- What moves you? Why?
- Which of the following makes you feel better: to give or to receive? Why?
- In what situations do you feel envy? Why?
- Identify situations in which you specifically seek to suffer. Why?
- In which situations do you use spiteful or sarcastic language? Why?
- In which situations do you behave frivolously? Why?
- Do you care a lot about other people's opinions? Why?
- When do you try to handle, control, or dominate people? Which people cause you to try to do this? Why?
- When do you feel anger against men? Why?
- When have you felt other women as your rivals? Why?
- When do you feel sorry for yourself? Why?
- When do you lie? What do you wish to achieve with this?
- What do you expect from life?
- What do you expect from a man?
- What do you expect from yourself?
- What things hurt you deeply? Why?
- What are you afraid of? Why?
- What are your main sexual fantasies? Analyze them.
- What causes you the most anguish? Why?
- Are you afraid of growing old? Why?
- What do you feel when you realize that you have attracted a man? Why?
- What is your attitude regarding sex? Why?
- Do you believe that people like you or reject you? To what do you attribute this?
- Are you happy being a woman or would you have preferred to have been born a man?

⦁    Are you satisfied or dissatisfied with your own life? Why?

These guidelines are only meant to shed some light on the areas that are useful to pay attention to, understanding however that in reality everything is important, and nothing should be discarded because, if something exists, it has a place in the inner world.

Hate, fear, vanity, concupiscence, ambition, destructiveness, love, tenderness, courage, loyalty, treason, avarice, detachment, correctness, incorrectness, intelligence, shrewdness, obtuseness, and shortsightedness, are all common elements of the human inner world and should not be ignored.

It would be a serious mistake and waste of time to answer the above questions in a direct, matter-of-fact way, since the questions are merely guidelines to show how a woman can become aware of these sensations inside of herself. The process is slow and gradual and it is therefore impossible to answer such questions all at once. The solutions will come about spontaneously and naturally through self-observation, dedication, and over time. Moreover, becoming conscious of one's inner world is not a finite activity; on the contrary, it requires continuous discovery and striving, thus guaranteeing uninterrupted growth.

A woman can fertilize herself through her psychic uterus with the sperm of her own conscious intelligence, and afterwards conceive herself and give birth to herself as an authentic woman. This is the only possible way for a woman to become truly emancipated and to put an end, through her own will, to female discrimination.

The person who feels humiliated has allowed this to happen internally because otherwise no external circumstance would be able to humiliate one. In the same way, discrimination is only possible when a woman allows it to occur by refusing to grow and develop. When she is effectively able to achieve a mature individual identity, there is no force in the world that can discriminate against her.

Remember that the main characteristic of the psychic function of the uterus is the capacity to transform and to conceive a new life. This capacity allows women to develop individually.

I cannot insist enough that until women assume responsibility for their own destiny, authentic realization will not be possible because authentic realization is the result of deliberate action carried out through willpower. It is an internal phenomenon, not an external one, even though it makes use of everyday experiences as the raw material for internal work.

Remember that the main objective of self-observation and of one's experiences is to create reflective consciousness, criteria, and discernment that emanate from one's "I." The meaning of the experiences is what gives one the ability to discern.

One must abandon rigid and unchanging formulas for the development of women, to avoid memorization and blind imitation which would make authentic evolution impossible. This is why the path is truly individual. Even though many women may come together to work, each one must do her work individually.

## CLEANSING ONE'S CONTAINER

During the process of becoming aware of one's inner world, a woman must also *cleanse her own container*, that is, purify herself from the psychic waste projected onto her by the social entity. Human passions, vices, and capital sins, are all forces that lie within the collective unconscious of humanity, and are projected into the psyche of each individual, invading and contaminating it.

Female sexuality is directly related to the limbic system. Therefore, a woman's emotions have a great impact on the excitation of her eroticism. That is why it is easy for a woman to fall prey to sadism or masochism because her imagination becomes activated by daring stories or morbid experiences.

Emotions and thoughts which have caught the negative social influence also contaminate the flow of one's libido. The libido is nonspecific in and of itself and obeys impulses received by the individual's psychic state.

By establishing control over feelings and thoughts, it is possible to decontaminate and sublimate the libido, since the activity of a person's vital forces will obey, to a certain extent, reflective and developed consciousness.

One can purify one's libido through correct management of one's emotional states and imaginative pictures, bringing it back to its original nonspecific condition. This can be done through adequate imaginative and emotional hygiene and using one's will to turn attention away from morbid things. Very often, people are very attracted to morbid and unhealthy things, and inadvertently get used to enjoying such morbid sensations and even unconsciously seek out situations that stimulate them. The tabloids exploit this particular human trait by highlighting sensational and passionate events.

It is only possible to understand the immense damage caused by these circumstances when one comprehends that all stimuli are sexual because sensitivity resides in the libido. This explains how imaginative and emotional sensationalism directly excite eroticism and create a perverse form of enjoyment. This also explains the great erotic pleasure that gamblers feel when they gamble. Gambling intensely excites the libido by alternating feelings of pain and pleasure coming from the expectations of winning or losing.

Therefore, women also need to habituate themselves to imagine and think only in positive and healthy terms, to close their minds to pornographic, morbid, and sensationalistic elements. This process needs to be one of choice, not of repression. In truth, a person would ingest contaminated foods only if that person ignored the fact that the food was contaminated or if the health repercussions from eating that food were not known. No one would be crazy enough to feed themselves with meat that has trichinosis, for example, but people contaminate their psyche every day by trapping destructive or unclean ideas in their imagination.

When a person realizes the immense damage that such negativity does to oneself, one might be able to find the adequate motivation to institute a degree of control over functions that are normally involuntary. It is essential to acquire the discipline necessary to keep one's attention away from thoughts and feelings that are dirty, corrupt, or sinful, and make sure that one's thoughts and feelings are a faithful expression of the reflective consciousness that one is trying to form.

It is not very difficult for a person who is used to dealing with one's inner world to selectively choose thoughts and emotions because the development of one's "I" allows one to have a greater degree of self-control. To have self-control is a sign of having a high degree of mental organization and an ability to organize one's mind hierarchically.

Thinking and feeling must stop being subliminal activities and become instead faculties that select the material to be accepted within. It is absurd to believe that one must forever remain at the mercy of social circumstances, open and defenseless to advertising or adverse, corrupt, and destructive mental influences. If that were the case, the human race would be more android than human.

Women have great reasons for learning how to be able to choose with their minds and close their imaginations and feelings to negative influences. This ability depends on the proper development of a woman's "I," which in turn must be formed through reflective meditation within her inner world. The "I" feeds from everyday experiences and transforms them into meaning. Therefore, the ability to discriminate consciously is an ability that must be encouraged, not shunned.

When there is a lack of control over one's imagination and emotions, one's psychic defenses are opened and permit all stimuli to indiscriminately enter into the psyche. When this occurs, one runs the risk of receiving all kinds of corrupt influences.

As part of the work to fight against the morbidity and sensationalism that wrongly excites the libido, women need to fight the bad habit of criticizing negatively or destructively for the sake of talking. It is also important to keep a lid on the anxiety of wanting to tell the latest spectacular news to one's friends, since the unconscious intention of this habit is to co-create excessive stimulation and emotional impact with them.

These recommendations do not constitute a moral judgment, or a set of mandatory guidelines. They are merely an objective warning and description of phenomena that are simple to prove. For example, the recommendation about not smoking is not a moral judgment, but rather a warning against a potentially carcinogenic activity, which has been clearly identified and proven. The same goes for all that is written in this book. My intention is not to reprimand, criticize, or disqualify, but rather to point out reality to all those who seek it. What each woman does with this knowledge is a matter that only concerns her. It is my sincere hope that the message is understood and evaluated properly because I believe that the evolution of women is the only possibility for positive change for humanity. The destiny of the world is undeniably in their hands.

To complement the process discussed thus far I recommend practicing an exercise that appeared in my book, *HypsoConsciousness*. If practiced correctly, the exercise of the *Mental Void* not only increases self-control but greatly increases the will's influence over one's thoughts and imagination.

### The Mental Void

There exists a real relationship between the eyes and the imagination. In order to create a mental void, one must start with the relaxation of one's eyes. The best way to learn the technique of this exercise is to tackle it in three stages as described below:

### Stage I:

Sitting comfortably or lying on your back, close your eyes and begin to focus your attention upon them. After a while, you will notice contractions and movements of your eyeballs and a tendency to blink continuously, despite the fact that your eyes are closed. By using your will, you should try to stop the slight fluttering of your eyelids and the muscular tension of the eyes.

Persevere until you observe that all the nervous activity in both eyes and eyelids has disappeared. This ends the first stage.

## Stage II:

Now, move your attention from your eyes to your breathing; that is, feel each inhalation and exhalation, trying to identify with the slight movement of the expansion and contraction of the chest.

Clearly feel the alteration of breathing in and out, in and out, in and out. You should NOT breathe deeply, just breathe normally.

## Stage III:

After a while, when you feel that you have reached perfect identification with your breathing, continue breathing but shift your focus to the imaginative visualization of the color black, which should continue until it vanishes.

The whole exercise must be practiced in a state of total immobility, maintaining the body as inert as possible. One must take as much time as one needs at each stage before passing on to the next. One should not proceed to the next stage without having mastered the former. The third and last stage can be prolonged for as long as one feels is needed, even if one falls asleep at the end.

When one attains the mental void, one should be feeling absolutely nothing. Perception is completely paralyzed. The feeling that approximates the state of being in the mental void is that in which time is standing still and one is suspended in the present moment which is timeless, motionless, and perception-less.

The habit of adequately relaxing one's eyes, which is described in the first stage of the exercise, can be employed throughout the day as an aid to controlling one's thoughts. After very little practice, one should notice a difference.

These exercises are not magical formulas for women to become truly feminine; instead, they are useful tools designed to help one to learn about and develop one's internal world, cleanse and sublimate one's libido, and obtain greater control over one's thoughts. What each woman gets from them depends entirely on how she uses them since these exercises are invaluable because of their significance, not their mechanical practice. The person who understands has everything; one who practices without understanding and merely repeats empty formulas, is a simple automaton.

# MATERIAL CIRCUMSTANCES

The female role has changed constantly throughout history, and yet, other than the role of motherhood, women's roles in society are still not very clear today. On the one hand, many women continue to follow traditional cultural patterns, and on the other hand, women currently have concrete alternatives that contradict traditional roles.

The following questions are still challenging for women today:

- Should I develop myself as a person or just concentrate on getting married?
- Should I be myself and show interest in aspiring toward something different, or should I just pretend to be less intelligent than a man?
- Should I work fulltime or only take care of the home?
- Am I failing as a mother in not giving my children the time they demand because I am too busy with my career?
- If I devote all my time to taking care of the home, will this not endanger the stability of my marriage because I might seem less attractive to my husband?
- If the children are sick, should I take care of them or go to work?
- If I try to be attractive, am I unnecessarily provoking my husband's jealousy?

This is just a short list of how one's material life is always in a state of flux, which can constantly create problems of some sort. Nevertheless, one needs to view such problems as enabling personal growth if managed correctly, not as something to be avoided.

In many women their mood depends on the presence or absence of problems, as if an absence of problems were a precondition for happiness. Such women live waiting for specific conflicts to be resolved as a requirement to initiate joy. This is nothing but a mirage because new difficulties will appear even faster and more often than the ones that have disappeared. Only the fetus lives in Nirvana—an environment that is ever nurturing, constant, and welcoming.

When people are too attached to the period in the womb, their concept of happiness is based on the absence of material difficulties. Such attitudes weaken character and will, since a person can get used to running away from obstacles or passing them over to others. Obviously, such childish behavior limits one's possibilities because one will not develop the necessary strength to forge an individual path in life.

On the other hand, it is more mature and healthy to be conscious of the fact that there will always be problems, and that life is like an obstacle course. Indeed, it is a big mistake to chase after external happiness based on material circumstances. A person is considered to possess intelligence when he or she knows how to take advantage of obstacles to increase personal development. Difficulties do not hinder happiness; it is the way one handles them and the significance and resonance they have in the person's internal world that counts. This is the case for some people who immigrate to another country seeking a favorable change in their lives but remain as miserable or unhappy as before, even though they are no longer plagued by their previous material problems. This shows how conflicts are *within* a person and one does not change by moving to another place.

Everything is a matter of internal attitude. It is so important not to be frightened by failure or setbacks. On the contrary, it is necessary to learn the art of life through them. In fact, living is an art that every woman should learn. Living, for women, refers to conscious, feminine, positive, and wise behavior.

To have wisdom in life means to be able to take advantage of all our experiences since they contain nutrients for our growth. Problems are not *bad*. The idea that problems are bad is a myth that has to be done away with. Problems are simply hurdles to overcome. It is in a person's hands to determine whether these problems are destructive or constructive. If one lets oneself get overwhelmed by these problems, one can be emotionally or physically destroyed by them. However, if they are handled positively, one will be nurtured and will grow. A person gathers strength and evolves by facing one's difficulties. When one does not face them, one grows weak and becomes diminished.

This is even more so for women who, in order to grow, must face conflictive situations to stimulate personal growth and strength.

Female weakness is evident when women worry too much about the future, when they try to determine or predict it, or when they contemplate external influences to save them, instead of deliberately shaping their future with their own internal resources. Many women live waiting for amazing and favorable events to occur, and they look down on simple everyday existence. According to the law of probability, the list of favorable events cannot be that numerous.

What happens with the rest of a woman's life if her life's meaning comes only from the short list of favorable events? It will regrettably have been wasted since she will have spent her time waiting for the next favorable event to occur. Meanwhile, she languishes in her everyday routine not realizing that this routine reflects what is really happening within her. Routine is within not without. All that is external occupies a space that corresponds to it in nature and follows nature's cyclical periods of rising and falling.

When a woman develops her internal world, she cannot get bored or fall into a routine because her inner space might be so vast as to need millions of years to explore and discover its riches.

Loneliness and anguish, problems that frequently affect women, always stem from internal lacking, that is, from the emptiness of their inner world. The void, in the sense used here, refers to a lack of conscious content where only unconscious elements, over which there is no control, remain. In fact, in the void unconscious elements govern the individual.

Another fundamental element that causes anguish and loneliness has to do with the lack of structure of a person's free time. I refer to the way in which people believe that each and every moment of their lives needs to be structured or spent doing something. When a person stops working or doing physical activities a great deal of time becomes available, and time can seem immense and threatening like a desert where the "I" feels absolutely helpless and unprotected.

Another element in women that causes anguish, is the feeling of uncertainty because when a woman does not trust herself she will logically expect everything to come from outside. These external resources are inevitably subject to life's ever-changing circumstances, and are, therefore, most uncertain.

It is so necessary for women to use their time fruitfully and constructively instead of wasting it with idle chatter, which does not help them develop or find themselves. Confidence and security are the benefits of structuring one's time. In turn, such confidence helps develop new, special skills that will enrich a person's life.

Unhappiness and discontent are often the result of self-disillusion when one is convinced that one has acted correctly but has not taken advantage of opportunities for self-realization.

A woman who is well-rounded, mature, and adult can overcome all material contingencies. She can do so because of the firmness, strength, persistence, and constancy of her "I"—her center of psychic identity that creates its own internal circumstances in her psychic uterus.

The effects of material events are not carved in stone. How they are handled is important. As long as a woman continues to make royal jelly out of her everyday experiences, she will continue to grow and develop constructively, no matter what difficulties she may encounter on her path. It is therefore fundamental to analyze one's everyday personal experiences, consciously reflecting on them, practice introspection and comprehend the significance of the events one has lived. The meditated significance of events is food for the "I," and a fundamental factor in creating inner strength.

Women have no idea of their own power. Indeed, except for nature, no other similar force exists in the universe. This refers to the ability that a woman has of interjecting and positively processing and transforming elements by means of the psychic function of her womb. Since nothing can withstand this alchemical process, women really do possess within the most powerful weapon to solve any problems or difficulties that show up in life. They only need to learn to use the YIN power of which women are made: yielding, adapting, welcoming, enveloping, encircling, persuading, and transforming.

The woman who behaves as a common female is a slave to events; an evolved woman, on the contrary, can determine her destiny through her individual actions. She does not need to adopt roles in order to have an identity or to define a place in society. In fact, her role and place in society must be defined by her. This can occur when she possesses an adult, conscious, and stable "I." She will then be able to reconcile her individual interests with social ones, keeping her femininity fully protected and nothing will be able to destroy it. She will be able to carry out the role she chooses above and beyond historical changes because her identity will be emanating from her inner world, not from social circumstances.

It will not matter if she is single, married, separated, whether she has children or not. A woman who obtains her psychic feminine identity will always have only one role: the feminine role.

One might argue that definitions change and that what is appropriate and relevant today might not be so in the future. However, just as history has not questioned a man's virility over time, so nature's laws remain intact despite the passing of time, and if it were possible to seriously disrupt nature, the universe would have already been destroyed. No social or scientific revolution can alter the fact that a woman has a vagina and a uterus whose psychic function corresponds to its biological activity, which is to receive and transform. Thus, the essence of femininity is a constant too.

Nothing and no one can abolish a woman's right to develop individually within her internal world and to build her own psychic means for self-determination. Self-determination will help her resist external changes, take them in, and transform them, not deny them.

Similarly, nothing and no one can stop a woman who, due to her own development, has become completely emancipated from the discrimination she faced previously, and has become equal to men by her own decree, not because of an externally ordained special law.

It also will not matter what profession she seeks to follow. Even if she is in a profession or job traditionally performed by men, she will still be able to preserve her femininity because she will no longer be at the mercy of external influences.

Stereotypically, women are expected to be: dependent, passive, soft, sweet, submissive, sentimental, affectionate, intuitive, fragile, superficial, protected, impulsive, self-sacrificing, and cowardly. None of these qualities are related to the individual capacity to reach one's goals. With only a couple of exceptions, these qualities correspond to a role implemented by and for men, turning women into useful appendages for them. Through this traditional role, a woman is expected to simply fulfill the role of motherhood or provide for a man's needs.

A woman who has fully developed herself does not fulfill the female role ordained by cultural conditioning, imitation, influence, and/or unconscious conditioning. Rather, she develops an individual feminine identity by working with her reflective consciousness in her internal world.

To achieve this, a woman does not require a professional title or need to be an intellectual, but she does need to learn how to think because she must form her own behavioral guidelines. These guidelines must be based on her own analytical criteria, not on stereotyped formulas. Furthermore, she needs to cultivate adequate emotional sensitivity to go with her new thinking because she will now possess a higher form of knowledge, which will have important ramifications in her interpersonal relationships. When she is able to put herself emotionally in the place of others, she will be able to communicate with others in a balanced way and avoid the kind of excesses that stem from narcissism.

A well-developed sensitivity also increases the power to understand, to receive and embrace ideas, facts, and concepts which might otherwise go by unnoticed.

The task recommended in this book is not for a select minority of women; it is offered to any woman who has already heard about these ideas. The only requirement is for her to have the sincere desire to improve within herself.

Despite the various stages in a woman's life—adolescence, the twenties, the forties, the golden years—and despite the many different possible scenarios—being rich, poor, cultured, uncultured, possessing varying ideologies and beliefs, professions, being single or married, with or without children, being happy or unhappy—absolutely every woman is capable of creating an evolutionary force inside herself that will help her achieve goals and attributes equal to any man. Any woman can decide to stop waiting for material events to make her happy. Any woman can stop waiting for her luck to change or for destiny to become more favorable.

Any woman can stop dreaming of catching the right man. In fact, she could accept to be with a regular man and help transform him from a dull man into a good companion. It is possible to stop dreaming about Prince Charming, famous men, movie stars, rich tycoons, or special individuals. A woman can learn to love without the interference of her own idealized image. (According to Reik, human beings bestow an idealized image onto the opposite sex to use that person as a hangar for their illusions.)

A woman who has developed herself will also be able to free herself from female stereotypes. She will no longer be concerned with the lives and biographies of famous women. She will not need to study the existential themes in the lives of famous or attractive men, and pit her strength against theirs, imagining that she is their complementary love object, which, under the circumstances, would mean that she would again be playing out a role determined by men and not by her, once again denying herself an authentic role.

A woman who has developed herself will not need to seduce important men to climb up the social ladder. Nor will she be compulsively enslaved to the cult of the body because she will have substituted this slavery with the cultivation of her soul.

After reading these paragraphs, many women might ask: "Then, what will we live for? What will we do if we can no longer dream and fantasize and have such expectations?"

Obviously, each woman will do what she desires to. If a woman would rather spend most of her time dreaming, she is as free to do so, as she is also free to renounce her sterile and unproductive fantasies and replace them with concrete realities.

There are two types of fantasies: one that is damaging, destructive and unproductive, and another that is creative. The former is a type of daydreaming in which one imagines situations through a state of comfortable stupor, never putting ideas into practice, and always waiting for them to become real through some kind of magic or by the grace of an external force. Such individuals lack the necessary courage, energy, and decision to *take heaven by force*. Their entire lives can be reduced to the words: *waiting for*—waiting for everything to come out of nothing.

Therefore, the apparent dilemma facing most women is: "Do I wait for society to guarantee legal equality albeit unreal with men? Or do I earn this privilege through my own effort?"

Unfortunately, it is well-known that millions of human beings waste their lives by constantly dreaming about what they want, without taking the required action to obtain it.

A woman who has developed herself fully need no longer depend on favorable or adverse material events. She can build her own destiny, regardless of what lies along the way.

A woman who is not deemed beautiful by society cannot rely on her physical beauty to stand out as an erotic object, and she is very often condemned to fulfill the maternal role or to imitate men. However, I assure you that when a woman possesses a rich inner world that is abundant in YIN energy, her inner beauty can successfully stand in the place of physical beauty.

Individual development does not mean that one has to completely relinquish fantasies or illusions; rather, it means one needs to use them intelligently and constructively. One must become convinced that it is more profitable to invest time and effort in one's inner world than in one's physical appearance. In fact, everything that is related to material values is easily destroyed, is ephemeral, and perishable, just like physical beauty, youth, and also economic power. I am not suggesting that one repudiate material values; rather it is convenient not to depend on them because they are possessions that diminish with age, and if one is overly attached to them, they transform the process of growing old into torture. In the end the message is not about living for physical appearances or for the frivolous and ephemeral gratification of one's own narcissism, which really wears one down and is unproductive and sterile vis-à-vis one's personal development.

One's internal world, on the other hand, does not decrease with age. Instead, it grows and becomes further enriched; it becomes part of the individual's being. It is not a possession that can easily disappear.

Clearly, when women will have changed, the role of men will also have to change because men will be forced to relate to women according to a different set of rules. Men who believe that women are weak, dependent, unintelligent, superficial, frivolous, and irresponsible will be tested. At first it might take them a while to adapt to a partner who now no longer behaves like a primitive female, but who has raised herself to the category of woman, with an individual psychic identity that is free, intelligent, strong and dynamic, and at the same time, intense and superiorly feminine. Perhaps many men will feel diminished in their masculine pride and vanity. If so, they will gradually need to get used to considering their companion as a person, not an object.

On the other hand, the relationship between the partners of a couple should improve since the relationship will be based on equality and not be a relationship of a protector with a kind of adopted daughter. It is well known that men fear the emotional dependence of a weak woman who psychically clings to them. This will not occur when men and women are on equal footing in a relationship. When men and women have achieved similar levels of development, they can only complement each other harmoniously and in a balanced manner.

My aim is to show women the great opportunity they have *right now* to be definitively, authentically, and irreversibly free, and to be able to decide their lives autonomously. This is a concrete and realistic opportunity, not a fairy tale. I sincerely hope that they will not choose childish stories over objective reality, and that they will decide to take advantage of this new and different perspective.

I dare to anticipate that if women agree to take advantage of this new perspective, they will reach a level of individual realization that will allow them not to rely on temporal reality, but to be able to create their own reality according to their individual yearnings. This will represent a definitive emancipation from male tutelage and offer women the chance to grow up and discover thousands of new and fascinating possibilities for development and fulfillment.

Then women will no longer depend on the role of motherhood to have proof of their own femininity. As a woman gives birth to herself through her psychic uterus, she will be able to educate her children wisely if she opts to have them, allowing them to develop their maximum potential and not be mere instruments of their mother.

Women will be allowed to train themselves to fulfill roles of greater prestige and relevance in society as a man's equal. They will be perfectly feminine, even when they carry out roles of authority and command because instead of issuing commands, they will convince others of the need to do as they ask. They will command through the YIN force, not the YANG force.

They will be able to consciously assume the role of *mothers of the world*, as they will lay the foundation for a better humanity because they will be able to give their children or their students that which they have achieved within themselves.

Men should progressively become less violent and more balanced as they feel complete in their relationships with women as their inner needs are calmed and fulfilled by women who in full femininity will be able to give and receive harmoniously. Furthermore, a man's intellectual capacity might increase considerably since it will now be complemented by his companion's feminine mind, thereby doubling their range of perception and comprehension.

If new generations form a reflective consciousness that is profoundly humane and able to overcome unconscious animal impulses it is not utopian to conceive of an end to all wars.

Throughout the centuries, human beings have been unable to change their inner natures in an evolutionary sense, and much of the blame for that lies with discrimination against women, who have hitherto not been encouraged to become conscious individuals. Instead, society had tried to turn them into a biological tool that produces intelligent human bodies that lack a reflective consciousness. The world has overlooked the crucial evidence that it is mothers who shape and educate babies, but who have been doing so without absolutely knowing how to accomplish it in a truly assertive and conscious manner.

Unfortunately, most women are bad mothers, not in a moral or affective sense but in a technical one since they are not developed or self-fulfilled individuals and are therefore unable to properly guide their own children. A person who has nothing can give nothing. This has been the sad reality of motherhood for many centuries and children have developed according to their mothers' compulsive needs. This still happens today all over the world and it is absurd when one comes to think of it since we are in a period that is supposed to be of immense progress!

I am reminded of the story of a mother hen that is raising a baby duck trying to turn it into a chicken at all costs without stopping to see its natural and individual aptitudes.

It is of great urgency that women are taught to be good mothers. But to do so they must have a foundation of self-fulfillment and development otherwise they will simply apply mechanical formulas. Social formulas, lest one forget, are for the masses not for individuals.

Social formulas produce only more unconscious masses not individuals. Only a fulfilled mother with a higher form of discernment can educate her children individually and give priority to the aptitudes and difficulties of each individual child.

When women become mothers to themselves, to their children, and to the world, humanity will have been sublimated in the psychic uterus of the female sex thus enabling social progress and the development of the human being's inner nature.

How many years must one wait for this to happen?

*The answer also rests with women.*

# APPENDIX

## ANALYSIS OF THE SURVEYS

The following surveys were created according to the author's guidelines, not according to rigorous and formal scientific criteria. It was the author's intent to discover if women know how they differ from men in non-genital aspects of their femininity.

130 women were interviewed from all socio-economic levels:

Twenty-eight from a lower socio-economic level (Group A)
Seventy-one from a middle class socio-economic level (Group B)
Thirty-one from a higher socio-economic level (Group C)

The author focused his interest primarily on the answers to questions: 1, 2, 5, 6, 7, 8, 12, 15, 18 and 19. Those questions are:

Q1:     What do you believe is the highest aspiration or goal that a woman can achieve in her life?

Q2:     What do you think are the main differences between men and women?

Q5:     What words do you associate with femininity?

Q6:     What fantasies or emotions arise in you when you think of your uterus?

Q7:     Do you think that the uterus could have a use other than for gestating and developing a human embryo? Give reasons for your answer.

Q8:     Would you have preferred to have been a man, or are you content with being a woman?

Q12:    Is there a woman you admire as a female role model from the past or from the present?

Q15:    In your opinion, what do you believe a woman's role is in today's world?

Q18:        What is the reason women give for having children?
Q19:        In your opinion, who has a greater chance of being happy in life, a man or a woman?

Here follows the analysis of each of the above questions:

## Q1:  What do you believe is the highest aspiration or goal that a woman can achieve in her life?

The main purpose for this question was to find out if women have transcendental values regarding an ideal model for feminine realization, that is to say, if they know how a woman who has achieved the most that she can should be, and what this "most" consists of.

Understandably, people build their lives according to the goals they want to achieve, so it can be very hard to overcome such pre-determined levels. If the maximum aspiration of an individual is to be a professional football player, for example, it is unlikely that he will become an intellectual or devote his life to the higher evolution of human beings.

People have ideal goals that might be their highest achievable point because they lack further aspirations. Thus, it is not possible to improve the moral and ethical level of humanity without first modifying its scale of values. As long as people do not aspire to higher goals that are aimed at benefiting humanity, world peace will remain a utopia and the evolution of one's internal nature will remain a mystery.

It is especially important to figure out a woman's ideal goals since it is women who shape future generations, passing down their own schemas.

The results of the first question were devastatingly poor, and reveal that the majority of women do not have transcendental values. Some answers are listed below:

"To make a home, have a profession, and have children"
(Employee, twenty-six years old, single, Group B)

"To have a home and children, yet be independent from the home"
(Cosmetologist, forty-nine years old, married, three children, Group B)

"To be a professional, to be independent, and to be a mother"
(Secretary, twenty-five years old, married, two children, Group B)

"Marry and have children"
(Housewife, thirty-five years old, married, two children, Group B)

"Become realized as a mother, wife, and professionally"
(Housewife, forty-four years old, married, two children, Group B)

"To grow as a person and be as happy as possible; to have a family and achieve a professional goal"
(Executive assistant, forty-nine years old, married, five children, Group B)

"To be successful in a profession, become realized as a woman, a mother and a wife"
(Secretary, twenty-two years old, single, Group B)

"Be a mother and have a normal home"
(Housewife, thirty-nine years old, married, two children, Group B)

"Have a family and make my husband and children happy"
(Housewife, thirty-nine years old, married, three children, Group B)

"Get a profession, be a woman, and a mother"
(Employee, forty-nine years old, married, two children, Group B)

"Feel fulfilled as a daughter, wife, and mother"
(Housewife, forty-eight years old, married, two children, Group B)

"The highest aspiration or goal a woman can have is to have children"
(Employee, thirty-one years old, married, four children, Group B)

"To find stability and be content with everything one has and does"
(Saleswoman, twenty-one years old, single, Group B)

"Have a good job and have children"
(Laundrywoman, thirty-three years old, married, two children, Group A)

"Find a good marriage"
(Hotel employee, thirty-eight years old, married, three children, Group A)

"To be a woman and to be a mother is every woman's goal"
(Home assistant, twenty years old, single, Group A)

"To have children"
(Teacher's aide, twenty-nine years old, married, two children, Group A)

"Marriage"
(Factory worker, fifty-six years old, single, Group A)

"To fulfill myself as a wife and mother"
(Home assistant, twenty-four years old, single, Group A)

"To have given love to those who are around us, mainly to children"
(Teacher, fifty-six years old, married, three children, Group C)

"Whatever one wishes"
(Teacher, twenty-eight years old, married, four children, Group C)

"Be a wife and mother"
(Accountant, forty-five years old, separated, Group B)

"Be a mother, a wife, and then develop professionally"
(Commercial Engineer, twenty-four years old, married, Group C)

"Become fulfilled as a mother"
(Doctor, twenty-eight years old, married, Group C)

"Be a mother and a professional"
(Psychologist, fifty-five years old, married, one child, Group C)

These answers are a random sample chosen from among all three socio-economic groups.

The answers show that the highest achievement that a majority of women envision does not have to do with their own development, but rather revolves around men. They are not able to perceive their own fulfillment individually and autonomously that will allow them to develop into individuals; rather, they limit themselves to marriage, children, and in some cases, to having a profession.

Having a home and children is for the man's benefit, and the yearning to become a professional often reflects the desire to compensate for a feeling of genital inferiority, which is hoped to be gained by performing a role of prestige. Once again, equality to men is using men as the reference point.

None of the answers had to do with self-referential goals regarding individual growth and development. None of the goals were purely and exclusively of the female gender, but were rather based on men. Almost all the answers had nothing to do with impersonal goals that transcend the personal "I" for the benefit of society.

Is it true then that when women only want to marry, have children, and have some activity or profession it is to compensate for their feelings of inferiority? The reason for this does not have to do with real inferiority, but rather with how women are socialized. They are socialized to ignore other valuable, significant, and important things that are worth desiring.

It is interesting to note that marriage is not visualized as a means to achieve some kind of specific fulfillment, but as a goal in itself.

If women only want to marry and have children, and occasionally a profession, and do not entertain loftier goals, one can only imagine the tremendous repercussions for the future of humanity.

**Q2: What do you think are the main differences between men and women?**

"I think that the difference has to do with gender, physical strength, and the mentality about being a man which boys are brought up with" (Saleswoman, thirty-four years old, single, Group B)

"I believe men and women are the same, but that in some countries men have better possibilities to achieve higher positions in the work environment" (Secretary, forty-six years old, married, one child, Group B)

"None" (Secretary, twenty-nine years old, single, Group B)

"Only gender and brute force that men have and women do not" (Saleswoman, twenty-one years old, single, Group B)

"More sensitivity in women; less possibility for professional growth" (Executive, thirty-three years old, married, two children, Group C)

"A woman's humanity is greater than that of men"
(Accountant, forty-one years old, widow, one child, Group C)

"I would say the differences are physiological and educational. I do not believe that there are great differences intellectually or emotionally"
(Programmer, twenty years old, single, Group B)

"Only gender"
(Housewife, thirty years old, married, one child, Group B)

"Different characters"
(Employee, fifty-four years old, single, Group B)

"Men are rough and domineering; women are submissive and obedient"
(Housewife, sixty years old, married, four children, Group B)

"Strength and the body"
(Secretary, thirty-one years old, single, Group B)

"For me it only has to do with hormones; there are differences among men and among women too"
(Housewife, forty years old, married, three children, Group B)

"Psychically, I would say no difference. The rest is not important"
(Secretary, thirty-four years old, single, Group B)

"One of the main differences between men and women is that men are cerebral and women are all heart"
(Telephone operator, twenty-five years old, married, two children, Group B)

"Men are chauvinists"
(Domestic employee, thirty-three years old, married, two children, Group A)

"I think that there is only one difference between men and women—gender"
(Housewife, twenty-two years old, single, Group A)

"Women belong more in the home and men are more free"
(Home assistant, fifty-four years old, single, Group A)

"Women are stronger than men"
(Housekeeper, thirty-nine years old, single, Group A)

"Different body shapes and the manner in which they express their feelings. Women cry often and men never do"
(Teacher, twenty-eight years old, single, Group C)

"The only difference is gender"
(Housekeeper, thirty-three years old, single, Group A)

"In our society, men are dominant and let themselves be loved. Women usually "give" although they like to be considered and received as well"
(Chemical engineer, forty-eight years old, separated, two children, Group C)

"Gender"
(Builder, thirty-four years old, single, Group C)

These answers seem to indicate that only external differences matter with regard to anatomy and, in some cases, behavior. Generally, there is such identification with the male gender that there is an inability to discern one's own identity with regard to personal characteristics and differences.

Women ignore their own condition when they cannot glean differences from men beyond anatomy.

As can be appreciated, the level of culture does not have great influence over this situation since the answers do not vary significantly across the economic levels.

Apart from gender, women do not know what it means to be a woman with regard to differentiating themselves from men.

In some answers there are attempts to compensate for a feeling of generic inferiority, and there seems to be little intention of clarifying the question, but rather to categorically state that equality between the sexes does exist. Therefore, the question seems to have been interpreted according to individual lacks.

**Q5: What words do you associate with femininity?**

"Sweetness, comprehension, fragrances"
(Secretary, forty-five years old, married, two children, Group B)

"Frankness, sweetness, cleanliness"
(Businesswoman, thirty-two years old, married, one child, Group B)

"Grace, good humor, tenderness, understanding, likeability, softness"
(Social Worker, forty-six years old, married, Group B)

"Careful, delicate"
(Housewife, twenty-six years old, single, one child, Group B)

"I don't know why but I associate femininity with clothes, hair, and learned facial expressions, for example."
(Executive Secretary, forty-nine years old, married, five children, Group C)

"It has to do with good manners, confidence and respectfulness"
(Accountant, twenty-two years old, single, Group B)

"Delicate, subtle"
(Housewife, thirty-three years old, married, four children, Group B)

"Tenderness, delicateness, motherhood"
(Interior decorator, forty-two years old, divorced, two children, Group B)

"It has to do with being a woman"
(Housewife, thirty-five years old, married, four children, Group B)

"Sweetness"
(Retired, sixty-two years old, separated, four children, Group B)

"Softness, patience, delicateness"
(Housewife, thirty-eight years old, married, three children, Group B)

"Soft manners, tenderness, coquettishness"
(Accountant, twenty-six years old, single, Group B)

"With being a woman"
(Housewife, thirty-seven years old, married, two children, Group B)

"With motherhood"
(Housewife, thirty-nine years old, married, three children, Group B)

"I associate it with women, clothing, jewelry, cosmetics, sweetness, coquettishness, motherhood"
(Housewife, fifty-one years old, married, three children, Group B)

"With manners and gestures, makeup and clothes"
(Secretary, twenty-one years old, single, Group B)

"Dressing femininely"
(Maid, thirty-two years old, married, two children, Group A)

"Delicateness"
(Housekeeper, thirty-three years old, single, Group A)

"With being a lady and well mannered"
(Teacher's assistant, forty years old, married, three children, Group A)

"Female, woman"
(Housekeeper, twenty-nine years old, married, one child, Group C)

"Delicateness, personal care; to know when to talk and when to be quiet"
(Teacher, thirty-four years old, single, Group C)

"Pink; affected"
(Builder, thirty-four years old, single, Group C)

"Delicateness, subtleness, grace, charm"
(Accountant, forty-five years old, separated, one child, Group C)

"Coquettishness"
(Food technician, twenty-seven years old, married, Group C)

"Perfumes, caresses, coquettishness, smiles"
(Professor, twenty-four years old, married, Group C)

"Delicateness, coquettishness, discretion"
(Nurse, fifty-seven years old, widow, one child, Group C)

"Has the essence of being a woman"
(Doctor, twenty-eight years old, married, Group C)

"Delicateness, softness"
(Nutritionist, thirty-one years old, single, Group C)

As we can see, femininity is associated with mostly external elements such as clothing, perfumes, manners, makeup, and motherhood.

The characteristic that is repeated most often is delicateness. Thus, femininity is linked to a condition of frailty or weakness and to repressed behavior. Other words such as softness, sweetness, and careful are expressions that seem to indicate a behavior that is incompatible with the need to show one's own emotions. Furthermore, these qualities have specific value for men or the beholder than for the person who possesses them. They also reveal the profound dependence of women on other people's opinions because the main reason for such qualities seems to be to project a good image.

It would be an ironic and sad joke to think that the Supreme Creator created such a limited creature if the main characteristic of women is to be frail and to make a good impression on others. Furthermore, most of us ignore true femininity and confuse it with erotic attraction, with being a "female" and being able to conceive children.

Only one individual out of all the women surveyed associated *femininity* with *a force,* and not with something external.

Some of the external characteristics cited had to do with: having long hair, being slim, possessing a good figure, dressing elegantly, dressing femininely, being coquettish, being concerned with oneself, makeup, housework, beauty, caresses, smiles, etc.

A majority of those surveyed showed how totally ignorant they are of internal qualities when they simply responded that they associate femininity with "being a woman." Many others did not even answer and there were no major differences according to socio-economic levels.

How can a woman be feminine if she does not know what it is? How can a woman have her own identity beyond the role of motherhood?

Again we find that under these conditions women have adopted masculine roles in order to define themselves even if it is by imitating behaviors that correspond to the extreme opposite of their own condition.

One of the unique responses came from a woman who associated femininity with the color pink and with being affected, with the latter word referring to a kind of tackiness, extravagance, affectedness, and bizarreness. In this light, it would seem that femininity as such has never even existed on earth.

**Q6: What fantasies or emotions arise in you when you think of your uterus?**

"Regret for not having had more children"
(Cosmetologist, forty-nine years old, married, three children, Group B)

"That it can create another life"
(Employee, twenty-six years old, single, Group B)

"It is a sacred place for me"
(Secretary, twenty-five years old, married, two children, Group B)

"None, it is another part of the human body"
(Model, twenty-eight years old, single, Group B)

"I associate it with disease and operations to not have any more children"
(Saleswoman, sixty-five years old, widow, seven children, Group B)

"I see it as an organ with no emotions"
(Housewife, thirty-five years old, married, two children, Group B)

"None"
(Housewife, forty-four years old, married, two children, Group B)

"None"
(Accountant, twenty-seven years old, divorced, two children, Group B)

"Sensuality"
(Businesswoman, thirty-three years old, married, three children, Group B)

"Discomfort, rejection"
(Businesswoman, thirty-nine years old, married, two children, Group B)

"Loving emotions, associated with a nest where life is continued"
(Social worker, fifty-nine years old, widow, no children, Group C)

"None"
(Teacher, twenty-eight years old, married, four children, Group C)

"A warm, silent, and protected space"
(Teacher, thirty-six years old, married, two children, Group C)

"A place where my children lived without paying rent"
(Teacher, forty-one years old, married, three children, Group C)

"None, because I do not want children yet"
(Teacher, twenty-four years old, married, Group C)

"Fear of having cancer"
(Housekeeper, twenty-nine years old, married, one child, Group A)

"Nothing at all"
(Maid, forty years old, married, two children, Group A)

"Fear of having cancer"
(Maid, fifty-two years old, married, eight children, Group A)

"That it be healthy"
(Maid, thirty-two years old, married, two children, Group A)

The answers are basically divided into four types of responses:

- Showing no emotion at all
- Associated with motherhood
- Associated with sex
- Associated with disease or something unpleasant.

The four responses seem to indicate that women are afraid to think about having an inner space as part of their gender, so they prefer to ignore it, avoid it, relate it only to biological functions, or avoid thinking about it.

The rejection of this internal space indicates a lack of an inner world in its true meaning, and when it is described merely in terms of its biological functions, it is reduced simply to a primitive expression. There is almost no notion or concept of a psychic interior space. The only answer that comes close to its meaning talked about the uterus as "a warm, silent, and protected space."

A majority of women surveyed from the lower socio-economic group associated their uterus with cancer or fear of illness. This might be because women in this group perceive their own lives as restrictive and burdensome, which translated into threatening thoughts about their health.

**Q7: Do you think that the uterus could have a use other than for gestating and developing a human embryo? Give reasons for your answer.**

None of the answers to this question associated the uterus with a kind of internal world or with a place where strength resides.

To conclude, women feel empty and their uterine space painfully reminds them of a feeling of castration. That is why a woman becomes emotionally numb when she thinks about it, or, otherwise, she resorts to the well-known role of motherhood in order to relate to it.

**Q8: Would you have preferred to have been a man, or are you content with being a woman?**

Even though the question is very direct, the results were very interesting. The answers were so similar, that it would be redundant to cite them. Many answered as follows: "I am happy to be a woman." Indeed, it seems as though everyone had agreed beforehand to answer in a similar way because the wording of the answers was so exactly alike. Such stereotypical behavior represents a defense mechanism in the face of a bothersome or disturbing subject.

A small percentage answered that they would have liked to have been born a man in order to have had more freedom. This implies that such women envy men because men can be themselves, whereas women are social beings tied to convention and dependent on the opinions of others.

Some of the surveyed women reacted in an exaggerated manner by stating: "There is no way that I would ever have wished to have been born a man." Again, such a strong and violent defense implies exactly that they indeed would have preferred to have been born a man.

There is a high proportion of women who would have liked to have been born a man, but do not want to admit it to themselves because it would also mean recognizing that they are frustrated.

Some older women said, "I used to wish to be a man, but not anymore." This probably has to do with the fact that it would do them no good to recognize this desire at that late stage of life.

The feeling of inferiority with regard to men is clear, as well as the feeling of genital lacking that causes non-conformance with their own gender.

(Note: The answers to Question 11 are very similar to the answers given to Question 5, and are therefore not included.)

**Q12: Is there a woman you admire as a female role model from the past or from the present?**

A majority of women at the time of the survey answered that they do not have any female role models, which brought to light the absence of self-realized women as role models at the time of the survey.

Among the most admired role models of the past were Joan of Arc, Indira Ghandi, Gabriela Mistral, Margaret Thatcher, and Golda Meir.

It is significant that all these women were somewhat androgynous and not typically feminine. Rather, they represent women who imitated the masculine role. Joan of Arc, for example, is a clear example of the phallic or Amazonian warrior woman.

It is really contradictory that while some of the women who took the survey defined femininity in terms of long hair, thinness, one's figure, coquettishness, beauty, caresses, delicacy, frailty, weakness, and work in the home; the women they admire have very different characteristics. This seems to indicate just how terribly confused women are with regard to their own sexual identity insofar as its psychic or social role.

**Q15: In your opinion, what do you believe a woman's role is in today's world?**

"I believe that in today's world women must become part of society" (Businesswoman, forty-nine years old, married, eight children, Group B)

"To become fulfilled as a professional, wife, and mother" (Housewife, thirty-nine years old married, two children, Group B)

"To take care of her children and help her husband as much as she can"
(Seamstress, forty-four years old, married, two children, Group B)

"The same role as always, only with more support and more openly"
(Secretary, twenty years old, single, Group B)

"Be a man's companion"
(Secretary, forty-two years old, single, Group B)

"Be a woman, a worker, a mother, and a wife"
(Computer operator, twenty-six years old, single, Group B)

"Similar to men. Get ahead and achieve her goals in positive things"
(Student, twenty-six years old, married, two children, Group B)

"Become realized as a mother, a wife, and professionally"
(Housekeeper, twenty-four years old, single, Group B)

"A woman's role in today's life is to be a mother, wife, lover, companion, and professional"
(Accountant, thirty-three years old, married, one child, Group B)

"She must help and support her husband if she is married. Regardless of whether she is married or single, she must participate more in today's society"
(Bilingual assistant, thirty-six years old, married, three children, Group B)

"Be a woman"
(Housewife, thirty-one years old, married, three children, Group B)

"To help her husband as much as possible; to not demand more than he can give her, and to try economize as much as possible"
(Housewife, thirty-eight years old, married, four children, Group B)

"To be active"
(Employee, thirty-eight years old, married, three children, Group A)

"Create own home"
(Housekeeper, twenty years old, single, Group A)

"Educate her children and be useful to society through her work"
(Factory employee, forty-four years old, married, eight children, Group A)

"To try to make the roles of motherhood, wife, and professional as compatible with each other as possible"
(Accountant, thirty-one years old, married, two children, Group C)

"Just like any person, I believe that men and women have the same role: to work and to try to be happy"
(Teacher, twenty-eight years old, married, two children, Group C)

"Be able to have a harmonious family with a man"
(Nurse, twenty-four years old, married, one child, Group C)

"The role she has always had: mother and a man's companion, and also develop professionally"
(Commercial engineer, twenty-four years old, married, Group C)

"Daughter, mother, wife, professional"
(Professor, thirty-one years old, married, two children, Group C)

The answers point to a role that was made by and for men: in the home, motherhood, giving support to her husband, being a man's companion, etc. She has no role with regard to herself, but only with regard to a man. This confirms the definition of women as being the *daughter of, companion of, and mother of,* rather than possessing an individual feminine identity.

Many of the answers not reported here were vague and stereotypical, revealing either ignorance or lack of knowledge about the question being asked. Some of the answers state that a woman's role is the same as a man's, which of course, merely confirms the concept of women imitating men's roles.

Other than motherhood, there seem to be no defined characteristics regarding a woman's role per se. She may be defined as a female, but not as a woman. Her main activity seems to be to stay at home and help her man.

## Q18: What is the reason women give for having children?

"Because it is one of a woman's roles"
(Teacher, thirty-eight years old, married, four children, Group C)

"To have children, to educate and help them to live in harmony in this world brings happiness"
(Librarian, fifty-one years old, married, no children, Group C)

"The materialization of love for a man"
(Occupational therapist, twenty-four years old, single, Group C)

"Perpetuate the human race"
(Nurse, twenty-six years old, single, Group C)

"To be able to be more sensitive emotionally"
(Psychologist, fifty-five years old, married, one child, Group C)

"To follow a divine mandate, feel happy for being able to prolong life through the love between a man and a woman"
(Teacher, twenty-two years old, single, Group C)

"I do not think that motherhood is a purpose. Rather, it is a need born spontaneously when you love a person; that love is extended through children to whom we give everything they need"
(Librarian, thirty-three years old, married, three children, Group C)

"To create a home, give all that the fruit of love deserves, and become fulfilled as a mother and wife"
(Professor, twenty-nine years old, married, one child, Group C)

"Procreation and Love"
(Professor and researcher, thirty-nine years old, single, Group C)

"To truly feel like a woman and be proud of her children"
(Machine operator, forty-two years old, married, two children, Group A)

"To become realized as a woman"
(Laborer, fifty-six years old, single, Group A)

"To be a mother, wish to take care of her children and give them all that she can"
(Housekeeper, forty-six years old, single, Group A)

"When a woman has children she feels fulfilled as a woman and mother, then she understands her own mother better"
(Employee, fifty-three years old, married, one child, Group A)

"To feel like a complete woman"
(Housekeeper, twenty-four years old, single, Group A)

"Besides increasing the population, to become fulfilled as a woman, a mother and to take care of her children"
(Saleswoman, single, thirty-four years old, single, Group B)

"Become realized as a mother. Give one's husband continuity, and a reason to work. By materializing her love, a woman fulfills a natural law"
(Volunteer, forty-six years old, married, no children, Group B)

"To feel more complete as a woman"
(Housewife, twenty-six years old, single, Group B)

"More than anything else to become realized as a woman and know that from one's children another life can emerge"
(Employee, twenty-six years old, single, Group B)

"I think that a woman needs to have a child even without marrying; it is like the prolongation of one's own life, the fruit of what we are"
(Secretary, twenty-five years old, married, two children, Group B)

"Propagate the species and also feel fulfilled"
(Model, twenty-eight years old, single, Group B)

"Become a woman"
(Housewife, thirty-five years old, married, two children, Group B)

These answers seem to say that without children, women are castrated beings because they use their offspring to feel complete.

Without reproducing, women do not feel like women; they think they are only a fragment of what they should be. Motherhood is the only role that belongs to women exclusively and that grants them, therefore, a perception that they are overcoming their feelings of inferiority. Having children is fulfillment in terms of being a female, but not in terms of being an individually developed woman.

To be a mother does not define a woman as an individual. It does not define her individual identity. Rather, to be a mother only indicates that a woman is doing what the majority of women can do. In fact, other female animals *do* motherhood more perfectly and efficiently.

Therefore, being only a mother does not define a woman in her feminine dimension. Rather, it is a function of the female part of the species. An individual does not become fulfilled by doing something that is no different from what others do. It is clear that women have children to compensate for a feeling of inferiority and genital lacking, and not for self-realization. The subject here is discussed at the level of the individual not from the view of preserving the species.

It is opportune to keep in mind the correlation of baby to penis that psychoanalysis has established. In other words, at an unconscious level the baby symbolizes the phallus, and having a baby is how one obtains the desired penis.

The majority of answers to **Question 19** were so similar that there is little point listing them. However, the overall common factor seems to infer that the question itself frightens women. Certain responders to the survey answered the question with the word "both" in capital letters, and sprawled across the full width of the paper, followed by huge exclamation marks. This overreaction seems to indicate that most of the responders were rather startled by the question because deep down they most likely believe that men have greater possibilities for happiness, and this is something they do not wish to recognize.

In addition to the one word answer, some responders answered the question with disproportionately long answers, as if they were trying to justify at all costs that both genders have the same opportunities.

This type of answer also reflects that unconscious defense mechanisms were present.

In some answers, the responders stated that women have greater possibilities, but gave no further explanations.

Where the answer to the question was that both sexes have similar possibilities, there probably exists an unconscious desire to show that women, despite their "inferiority," have as many opportunities as do men. When reading the question, therefore, it would appear that the first thing that came to mind was a feeling of generic inferiority.

The author's hypotheses that were in place before the survey was conducted were confirmed fully and led to the following general conclusions:

- Generally, women lack truly transcendental values and only possess external values that are temporal and extremely limited.
- Women ignore how they differ from men other than with respect to physical characteristics.
- Women are terribly confused about their own sexual identity, and therefore imitate masculine roles.
- Women lack an inner world in the sense of having an interior space whose content is intelligent, under their control, valuable, and conscious.
- Women lack individuality. All women are defined by the same things. That is why women seek to stand out by having exclusive clothes or exotic looks.
- Women envy men's greater freedom, which they perceive as allowing them to be more themselves as opposed to women who are a social entity.
- When women are not mothers, they feel castrated.
- Women do not have any kind of individual self-realization based on transcendental values.
- Women lack transcendental goals.
- A woman's existence revolves around a man.
- Women do not know what femininity is.
- Women associate the concept of femininity with external values and social life. They do not associate it with a kind of energy that belongs exclusively to women.
- Women lack a stable, internal, feminine, and mature "I" that is constant. A woman's "I" changes according to circumstances.

Under no circumstances should these conclusions be interpreted negatively, nor should they be used as an argument to excuse or prove that women are inferior. As has been expressed continuously throughout this book, women are the result of external and internal circumstances, of historical and social circumstances, of a process of socialization designed for women to take on the role of motherhood and remain passive. When women plead inferiority to get protection from a man and become totally dependent on him, they prevent their individual development.

Because of the demands placed on men, they seem to have more individuality than do women, which allows them to remain anonymous. Men can be vulgar or crass without their self-esteem feeling diminished. Most men dress in the same way, with the same colors, same fabrics and styles because they are not looking for external exclusivity.

Since women feel more homogenous among each other than men do, their rivalry is easily understood because of their eagerness to stand out individually. When a woman compares herself to another woman, every other woman represents one possibility less for being original.

The result is that women have not really taken on the challenge of their own lives and prefer to remain in the shadow of men. Women who have assumed a feminist stance to defend their interests do so by fighting against men, not against their own weaknesses and lacks. Such women try to limit the male expansive force instead of developing their own energy and power. Thus, feminists are in reality still as dependent on men because the hormonal indicators that motivate their activities are rooted in men, and because they lack a self-referential attitude, they continue to use men as a point of reference for their fight.

It is my conviction that women are in no way inferior to men: it is the woman who places herself in a subordinate position, either because she wants to ignore her own capacities or because she wants to prolong the comfort of not having responsibilities that are too onerous.

I agree with those authors who believe that humanity is a whole; men and women are complementary opposites that together form a unity. The two genders, no matter how different, are made for each other and complement each other.

Women urgently need help to emancipate themselves from discrimination; they require full support and understanding by men, not in the form of new laws, but rather to launch their individual development. This task is essentially an individual task; that is, each woman must personally shoulder the responsibility for her self-realization. Self-realization is self-taught and is active. It is not the same as passively participating in a study group.

When women's groups are guided by instructors who are not trained to think consciously and reflectively, there can be rather negative consequences, in that a particular characteristic of groups of women is the ease at which a psychological mob forms. According to Gustave Le Bon, also confirmed by Freud, what accumulates in psychological masses is not talent, but rather mental poverty. If the instructor is ignorant of this phenomenon, the work can be very discouraging and of little help.

For this reason, the author insists over and over again on the individuality of this task. It is helpful to get together as a group provided the concept of individual responsibility is not diluted and remembering that progress will only take place as a result of personal effort, not because of more or less group work.

This book was written with the intention that it be studied with patience, attention, and care. It is not meant for a simple read through. Women need to take the time and reinterpret the feeling of being a woman, which is currently contaminated with feelings of inferiority and insecurity. Since emotions are the product of interpretation and not stimuli, they can be reinterpreted in order to imbue them with a higher positive meaning. This transition should not be based on mere caprice, but rather on rational objective evidence. That is precisely the reason why the author thought it necessary to bring forth the motivations of female behavior out of the darkness of the unconscious so that each woman—through understanding the hidden motives of her mistaken behavior—will be able to modify them in a positive manner.

The process is not one of recognizing how bad one is. Rather, it is a process of visualizing how much one can progress by letting go of the burdens that hinder personal development. This is how women can mobilize the enormous internal power that lies latent within them and that has remained inert until now.

Each reader needs to fully understand the immense power to transform that lies within one's psychic uterus as a woman. When this force is adequately employed, it can open the doors to one's freedom, self-development, and personal success.

Gradually comprehending the concepts within this book will in time allow women to reinterpret emotions associated with being a woman and grant them the certainty of the tremendous fortune that resides in their feminine sexuality. This conviction can only get stronger as women experience the proof of their material realizations.

The emotion of feeling disadvantaged by being a woman that usually accompanies all female beings should disappear in the light of the new interpretations and will be replaced with a concept of equality, autonomy and triumph.

* * *

The following variables were established for the survey that may help broaden the vision of this work.

## LOWER SOCIO-ECONOMIC GROUP (GROUP A)

Twenty-eight women were surveyed, with the following results:

The percentage of contentment or not with being a woman:

Twenty-three women (82.1 percent) stated that they are content with being a woman

Five women (17.9 percent) were not

*What is the biggest defect that women criticize within themselves?*
a.  Envy
b.  Alcoholism
c.  Vulgarity

*What is the worst defect that women see in men?*
a.  Male chauvinism
b.  Various vices
c.  Womanizing, selfishness, irresponsibility, hypocrisy

*The differences perceived between men and women:*
a.  Women are stronger and harder working
b.  Men are more cowardly
c.  Psychological differences
d.  Freedom and social roles

Six women (21.4 percent) see differences
Twenty-two women (78.6 percent) do not see any differences

*The most frequently found characteristics in an ideal man:*
a.  Loving
b.  Good-looking
c.  Understanding, hard working, sincere

*Motherhood:*
a.  Six women (21.4 percent) do not have motherhood as a goal
b.  Twenty-two women (78.6 percent) have motherhood as a goal

# MIDDLE CLASS SOCIO-ECONOMIC LEVEL (GROUP B)

Seventy-one women were surveyed

The percentage of contentment or not with being a woman:

Fifty-nine women (83.1 percent) stated that they are content with being a woman

Twelve women (16.9 percent) were not

*What is the biggest defect that women criticize within themselves?*
a. Lying
b. Envy
c. Selfishness
d. Jealousy

*What is the worst defect that women see in men?*
a. Male chauvinism
b. Infidelity and/or womanizing
c. Lying and Selfishness
d. Irresponsibility.

*The differences perceived between men and women:*
a. Women are more extroverted
b. Women are less cerebral
c. Women are more hard-working
d. Women are more docile
e. Women have a sixth sense
f. Women have more inner strength
g. Women are more mature
h. Women are more humble
i. Women are more realistic
j. Women are more imaginative
k. Women are more dependent
l. Women are less selfish
m. Women are more capable of making clear decisions

*Men:*
a. Men have greater possibilities in the work force
b. Men have greater brute strength
c. Men are domineering and male-chauvinistic
d. Men are calculating

e.  Men are dreamers
f.  Men have more freedom for action
g.  Men are more independent
h.  Men are more emotionally stable
i.  Men are weaker
j.  Men are intellectual

*Three characteristics that are most frequently repeated in an ideal man:*
a.  Affectionate and loving
b.  Hard-working
c.  Responsible and understanding

*Motherhood:*
a.  Fifteen women (21.1 percent) do not have motherhood as a goal
b.  Fifty-six women (78.9 percent) have motherhood as a goal

## HIGHER SOCIO-ECONOMIC LEVEL (GROUP C)

Thirty-one women were surveyed

The percentage of contentment or not with being a woman:

Twenty-six women (83.9 percent) stated that they are content with being a woman

Five women (16.1 percent) are not

*What is the biggest defect that women criticize within themselves?*
a.  Envy
b.  Selfishness and vanity
c.  Superficiality

*What is the worst defect that women see in men?*
a.  Male chauvinism
b.  Irresponsibility, selfishness, the belief that men are superior
c.  Lying

*The differences perceived between men and women:*
a.  Differences in social role of each gender
b.  Physical differences
c.  Psychological differences
d.  Capacity for love, feelings

*Three characteristics that are most frequently repeated in the ideal man:*
a.   Intelligence
b.   Loving
c.   Understanding

*Motherhood:*
a.   Six women (19.3 percent) do not have motherhood as a goal
b.   Twenty-five women (80.7 percent) have motherhood as a goal

Throughout this survey and across all three socio-economic groups, *envy* seems to be one of the defects that women recognize the most in themselves, and the worst defect attributed to men is *male chauvinism.* The two characteristics that are most desired in an ideal man are his abilities to be *loving and understanding.*

Almost 80 percent of women of all levels have motherhood as a fundamental goal.

With regard to envy, it is worth mentioning that in reality, it stands for resentment about the lack of a penis. This resentment is independent of whether its target is men or women. When the target is another woman, it is because the envied woman is a competitor in the game of catching a man, that is, to be able to have a controllable penis.

With regard to male chauvinism, it is important to point out the contradiction between how women responded in the survey and their real attitudes in life because it is really obvious that many women prefer male chauvinists.

Lastly, even though this survey was taken in Chile it is very likely that the answers—in their core significance—would not be much different in other countries, and if they differed, it would only be about surface characteristics.